# How To Stop Spending

## Learn Over 200 Ways to Save Money Fast and Gain Financial Freedom

## Included Books

Cheapskate Living And Loving It

Living Frugal And Loving It

Cutting Back And Loving It

Downsizing Your Life And Loving It

Spending Less And Loving It

Frugal Minimalism and Loving It

# Table of Contents

**Book 1: Cheapskate Living And Loving It**

**Introduction**

**Chapter 1: Saving Money on Your Grocery Bill**

**Chapter 2: Saving Money on Your Electric Bill**

**Chapter 3: Television, Phone, Internet, Cells and More**

**Chapter 4: And There Is More!**

**Chapter 5: Final Tips for You to Save Money!**

**Chapter 6: How to Get Out Of Debt for Good**

**Chapter 7: Frugal Lifestyle**

**Conclusion**

# Book 2: Living Frugal And Loving It

## Introduction

## Chapter 1: Looking At The Big Picture

## Chapter 2: Eating & Entertaining on a Budget

## Chapter 3: Health & Beauty Hacks to Save Money

## Chapter 4: Checking Your Financial Fitness

## Chapter 5: Targeting the Technology Cash Drain

**Chapter 6: Don't be House Poor**

**Chapter 7: Looking Good For Less**

**Conclusion**

# Book 3: Cutting Back And Loving It

## Introduction

## Chapter 1: Clutter vs. Necessity

## Chapter 2: Tips for Decluttering and Simplifying Your Living Space

## Chapter 3: Tips for Decluttering and Simplifying Your Personal Space

## Chapter 4: Tips for Simplifying Your Décor

## Chapter 5: Tips for Organizing Your Storage Areas

# Chapter 6: Tips for Simplifying Your Closets

# Chapter 7: Downsizing for Your Sanity

# Conclusion

# Book 4: Downsizing Your Life And Loving It

## Introduction

## Chapter 1: What is Too Much in Life?

## Chapter 2: Evaluating Need versus Want

## Chapter 3: How to Reduce Your Belongings

## Chapter 4: Cutting Back on Your Chore List

## Chapter 5: Simplifying Your Thought Life

**Chapter 6: Enjoying what Matters**

**Chapter 7: Loving Your Simple Life**

**Conclusion**

# Book 5: Spending Less And Loving It

## Introduction

## Chapter 1: The Makings of a Budget

## Chapter 2: Helpful Ways to Budget Money

## Chapter 3: Creative Ways to Save Money

## Chapter 4: Learning to Investigate Purchases

## Chapter 5: The Trick to Finding a Creative Budget

## Chapter 6: Looking Forward to the Future

# Chapter 7: Spending Less, Saving More

# Conclusion

# Book 6: Frugal Minimalism and Loving It

## **Introduction**

**Chapter 1: An Introduction to the Minimalist Lifestyle**

**Chapter 2: How to Get Rid of the Clutter in Your Home**

**Chapter 3: How to Have a Minimalist Wardrobe**

**Chapter 4: Minimalist Eating**

**Chapter 5: How to Declutter Your Life and Finances**

**Chapter 6: Gifts**

**Chapter 7: Minimalist Living in Everyday Life**

# **Conclusion**

© Copyright 2020 by _____Kathy Stanton_____ - All rights reserved.

This document is geared towards providing exact and reliable information in regards to the topic and issue covered. The publication is sold with the idea that the publisher is not required to render accounting, officially permitted, or otherwise, qualified services. If advice is necessary, legal or professional, a practiced individual in the profession should be ordered.

- From a Declaration of Principles which was accepted and approved equally by a Committee of the American Bar Association and a Committee of Publishers and Associations.

In no way is it legal to reproduce, duplicate, or transmit any part of this document in either electronic means or in printed format. Recording of this publication is strictly prohibited and any storage of this document is not allowed unless with written permission from the publisher. All rights reserved.

The information provided herein is stated to be truthful and consistent, in that any liability, in terms of inattention or otherwise, by any usage or abuse of any policies, processes, or directions contained within is the solitary and utter responsibility of the recipient reader. Under no circumstances will any legal responsibility or blame be held against the publisher for any reparation, damages, or monetary loss due to the information herein, either directly or indirectly.

Respective authors own all copyrights not held by the publisher.

The information herein is offered for informational purposes solely, and is universal as so. The presentation of the information is without contract or any type of guarantee assurance.

The trademarks that are used are without any consent, and the publication of the trademark is without permission or backing by the trademark owner. All trademarks and brands within this book are for clarifying purposes only and are the owned by the owners themselves, not affiliated with this document.

# Introduction

This book contains proven steps and strategies on how to Save Money, Live a Frugal Lifestyle and Enjoy Life Debt Free.

Today many people are struggling just to make ends meet but you do not have to be one of those people! With the tips you will learn in this book, you will be living the life you always dreamed of and doing it debt free! You are going to learn not only how to save money every single day, but you are going to learn my proven strategy on how to pay off all of your bills and get out of debt.

There are tips in this book for every single person and along with the tips you will find explanations on how to follow through, as well as how much money you will be able to save each year by following these tips. If you choose to implement just a few of the tips in this book, you will find yourself saving hundreds of dollars each year that you can put toward getting out of debt and staying debt free!

The frugal lifestyle is a great one, so don't feel like you are going to have to do without the things you love just to save money. I am going to show you how to enjoy all of the things you do right now but save as much money as you can in the process!

# Chapter 1

# Saving Money on Your Grocery Bill

Groceries are one of the largest bills that many of us have to budget for each month. It is not a luxury item that we can choose to live without, but there are tons of ways for you to save on your grocery bill each week!

1. Start clipping coupons. Every year companies send out millions of dollars worth of coupons, but only a fraction of them are used. If you take just one hour each week and start clipping coupons, you will find that you will be able to buy name brand foods for much cheaper than you would pay for even the store brands. At first, this is going to cost you a few dollars per week but in the long run it is going to pay off substantially.

   Now, I want to explain that along with our food we usually buy our household supplies as well as our toiletries, so that is going to be part of what you will save money on with coupons.

   The first thing you are going to do is to collect your coupons. You can print these offline or clip them out of your Sunday paper. There are even sites online where you can purchase inserts for as low as 25 cents each plus shipping. This makes it a lot cheaper than buying a Sunday paper, which usually runs about $2.50 on average.

If you have a large family to feed, you will be able to purchase multiple inserts to save you a ton of money. Now, many people will clip a few coupons and go out to the local store and use them right away. You are not going to do this. You are going to save your coupons for when there is a sale and stock up on that item for free or almost free.

You need to stock up enough of that item to get you through about 6 weeks, which is when the item will go on sale again. Here is an example that is using hygiene products, there was a specific brand name shampoo and conditioner that was on sale at my local store. The normal price was $3.50 per bottle but it was on sale for $2.50 a bottle.

I knew I had ten $5 off two bottle coupons, so I ended up getting 10 shampoos and 10 conditioners absolutely free. Another one that I just took advantage of was a very expensive lotion that was on sale at my store for $3.00 per bottle. I had ten $5 off two coupons which made them 50 cents a piece, but to top that off I had a coupon that gave me $5 off a purchase of $25 or more making 20 lotions absolutely free!

You can do this on food just like you can on body products, cleaning products, and laundry supplies. Wait for a sale, top it with a coupon and get the lowest price possible!

2. Grocery shop at your local dollar store. I am talking about your dollar store that sells everything for a dollar! They sell groceries there too. They also take coupons, which makes everything very cheap. For example, they sell cereal at my local dollar store. Cereal for a dollar is great, but throw a coupon on top of that and get it for 66 cents a box, now that is amazing!

3. Plan your meals each week and use your grocery store flyer to do so! Every week you should get your grocery store flyer in the mail, use this along with your coupons to decide what you are going to eat for the week. Write down all the ingredients you will need for you meals planning them around what is on sale.

4. Shop in your own pantry. This is a big one! So many times people do not realize what they actually have in their cabinets. Have you ever went to the store, saw something you thought you needed, bought it only to come home and find 3 of the exact same untouched product in your cabinet? Once you have created your list of all the ingredients you will need for the week, check your pantry to see if you have any of them already in there.

5. Cook once, eat three times. This is one of my favorites. Did you know that you could actually get three meals for a family of four out of just one chicken? This is how I do it; first, I boil the cut up chicken to make chicken and dumplings with. I remove all the meat from the bones after the chicken has boiled; use the stock to make my dumplings adding about 1/3 of the meat. Then, I put the bones and skin in the crock-pot to make chicken noodle soup stock. Finally, I am able to throw some barbeque sauce on the 2/3 chicken meat I have left and serve barbequed chicken sandwiches.

You can do this with tons of different foods and cut back on what you are paying for meat each week!

6. Find a local discount grocery store. Many people like to say that the food you are buying at a discount grocery store is no good and you will get sick if you eat it. That in fact is not true. Each week I load up my children and drive 50 miles to the closest discount grocery store. The reason is that I am able to literally triple my money I have budgeted for groceries. For example, I am able to buy whole frozen organic chickens for no more than $3. Now I have told you how we can make one chicken last three days, so it is costing me $1 a day for our chicken!

   You can purchase everything you need at a discount grocery store! They sell milk way cheaper than you will ever find at the grocery store and it is not out of date. They sell a 24 case of yogurt for 2 bucks! Check around and see if you have a discount grocery store near you, even if you have to drive a little ways, it is worth it because you will be saving more than you can imagine on your grocery bill.

7. So many times, we have leftovers after dinner and think nothing about throwing them in the trash. If you really want to save money, you need to rethink leftovers. Make them into something different, take them for

lunch the next day look at those leftovers as your money, don't throw your money away. There are even times I purposely make leftovers because I know we can eat it on another night or I plan to make it into something else. Another great thing my kids love to do is leftover day. We save what is leftover throughout the week, throw it in the freezer, then on Sunday have a buffet type meal with all types of choices. This ensures nothing goes to waste.

8. Stop snacking or allowing children to graze while they are at home. So much food can disappear if you allow your children to get in the pantry and eat whenever they feel like it. You need to set up a schedule because the fact is that children as well as many adults will eat simply because the food is there and they can.

9. Set a budget and stick to it. If you set a budget and stick to it you will learn very quickly how to stretch you money. I am not joking when I say stick to it. If you go shopping on Saturdays and run out of food on Thursday, you will learn how to stretch whatever is left in your cabinets and you will be much more cautious the next week.

10. Only go to the store once a week and go with a list. Never go in the store without a list of the items you intend to buy. If you do, you will find that you are over spending and not getting the food that you really need to prepare meals with. Take your list and don't allow temptation to overtake you. Never go to the store just to pick up one or two things once you have already done your weekly shopping. So many times, we go in looking for one or two items and come out with a cartload. If you forget something, make due or figure something else out, but do not go back into that store. If you absolutely have to go in, only take the amount of money needed to purchase the item you need. Leave the debit card in the car and grab a little cash.

# Chapter 2

# Saving Money on Your Electric Bill

Oh how we dread seeing that electric bill each and every month. There used to be times that I had no idea how much electricity I had used and felt completely helpless. That was until I received an electric bill that was more than my house payment last winter. I decided things had to change. Here are some changes you can make.

1. No more dryer! Did you know that you could lower your electric bill tremendously if you just stop using your dryer? In the spring, summer and most of the fall you can line dry your clothes outside. In the winter, you can purchase a cheap (usually around $5) drying rack for your house. These racks usually hold about one load of laundry each.

2. How many times have we been told that we should turn the heat down in our homes if we want to lower our electric bill? I was taught that you should turn it down, then if you get really cold, warm up the house and turn it back down again. Then a study came out by my local electric company that said do not set your thermostat at one temperature and leave it there unless you are going to be out of the house for several hours or are going to bed. What you can do is in the winter start with your thermostat at 68 degrees, if you are comfortable at that temperature drop it to 67. Continue to do this until you find the temperature that you just cannot stand. In my

house, we often have jackets, multiple layers or blankets on us in the wintertime.

In the summer, you want to do the opposite. Set your thermostat at 74 degrees and see how warm you can stand it. On the days that it is not extremely hot, open your windows, turn on the fans and let the summer air in your home. Most of the time during the spring and fall you should allow your windows to be open since the temperature outside is not too hot or too cold.

3. Check all of your windows and doors for gaps as well as around your baseboards if you have a basement. In older homes, this is where a lot of heat is lost and cold air comes in at. If you find gaps, fix them.

4. Close off the rooms that are not in use. Shut the doors to the rooms that no one is in. If the kids are in the living room, there is no reason to heat the bedrooms. If no one is in the bathroom, shut that door. This will keep the majority of the heat in the main part of the house near the thermostat, which will ensure your furnace is not over working and you are not wasting any heat. You can do the same thing in the summer!

5. Open your curtains in the winter and close them in the summer! Find the windows in your home that face the sun, when the sun is high in the sky, open those curtains in the winter, this will help heat your house. In the summer, it will heat your house as well so make sure you close the curtains.

6. Unplug everything! Did you know that while you sleep at night and all of your electronics are shut off, they are

still using electricity? Even that cell phone charger you leave plugged into the wall when your phone is not charging is constantly using electricity. When you finish using something, unplug it.

7. Wash your clothes in cold water. This will work for the majority of people, unless you have an extremely dirty job you should wash all of your clothes in cold water. If you have clothes that are very soiled, you should keep them separate from the rest of your clothing and wash them in hot water by themselves. You should also make sure to wash your whites in hot water at least once per month to ensure they stay bright white.

8. Remove some of the light bulbs! In my house, I have two chandeliers that hang from the ceiling, each of these takes eight light bulbs. In no way do we need eight light bulbs to light our rooms, so I only put two light bulbs in each one. True it does not have the same effect as all eight, but you will save money if you don't fill up your light fixtures.

9. Change your filters in your furnace/air conditioner every month to keep it from over working and to keep the air flowing.

10. If you have the choice between the microwave oven and your conventional oven, use the microwave, it uses 90 percent less electricity than the conventional oven. If you have to use the conventional oven open it up after you shut if off in the winter, you can use that heat that is trapped in there to warm your house.

# Chapter 3

# Television, Phone, Internet, Cells and More

I once found myself paying over $100 for my satellite bill, $70 for my internet, $60 for a home phone and over $100 a month for my cell phone. I was tired of wasting money on these things, so I made a few changes. Here are a few tips for you for saving money on these bills and more!

1. Cut out the satellite. There is no reason for you to pay that huge satellite bill each month, instead opt for Netflix or something like Netflix. Today there are tons of different programs you can choose from and they start at about $7 a month. Sure, you will be one season behind on the shows you watch, but really what does that matter when you are saving over $1,000 a year!

   Instead of using the video on demand service, wait and watch the movie later. There is no point in paying $5 to watch a movie once, when you can purchase it at a resale shop for $1 in just a few months and watch it whenever you want. Or just order it from Netflix. You can have your movie in the mail in just a few days!

2. The phone bill was also another huge issue for me as well as my internet bill. Now, of course you can cut these bills completely if you really do not need them, but I have to have them for my work. I went to my local phone company and talked to them about the price. I ended up being able to pay just $69 each month for both services instead of the $130 I was paying. If you don't need the internet for work or school, it is best to go ahead and have it and your home phone shut off and use only your cell phone for these services.

3. Speaking of cell phones, we can really run up a huge bill each month. The way I got rid of this bill was at my local Wal-Mart. Yes you heard me right. I went to Wal-Mart, picked up a $10 prepaid phone and started looking at plans. I do not need the internet on my phone since I have it at home, so I am able to pay $35 per month for unlimited talk and text. Now, if I needed the internet on my phone and did not have it at home, I could pay $50 per month for unlimited talk text and web. This is a huge savings over any contract you will get with a cell phone. The phones are just as good as the ones you get with a contract and you don't have to be stuck with some out of date flip phone. If you are looking to save money on your cell phone bill, check out the prepaid cell phones available in your area.

4. Consider working from home. This is a huge money saver. Before I worked from home, I had to pay a babysitter to watch my three children, I had to pay for gas to get back and forth to work and the list went on and on. Now my children stay at home with me while I work in my office, saving me over $1,200 a month plus gas and so on. Figure out if it is feasible for you to work at home and determine how much money you will save if you do.

5. Stop purchasing items you have to make payments on. If you are going to purchase a car, make sure you have

the cash to do so. The last car I purchased after searching for several hours online cost me $500. I sold my other car for $500 and paid cash for the one I own now. The car is not beat up or a rust bucket, it is a 94 Lincoln that runs like a charm. If you take the time to search for these deals, you are going to save a ton in interest in the long run.

6. Buy used and save the difference. Going along with not making payments on anything, stop buying everything brand new. Find used items and save your money. Six years ago I purchased a used washer and dryer. I am very picky about my clothes, so after 2 hours of scrubbing them out, I was ready to use them. I paid $50 total for both and they are currently in my laundry room doing a perfect job. Granted, I do not use the dryer often, but it is there when I need it. You can do this with all of your appliances, but you need to make sure you are getting a good deal. For example, I went to buy a used deep freeze. It cost $100, so I decided I wanted to compare prices with a new one and found I could get a larger one that was on sale at a local store new for $60. Don't assume just because it is being sold as used that you are getting the lowest price you can.

7. Cut up the credit cards and pay them off. I personally have never owned a credit card and I never want to. I watched my parents have to file bankruptcy due to overspending on credit cards. If you currently own a credit card, cut it up, call the company and see if they will lower your interest rate then start paying them off. Once they are paid off, do not apply for new ones. Live on what cash you have in your pocket and do not accumulate debt.

8. Consider quitting smoking and drinking. The average smoker spends over $150 each month on cigarettes and depending on how much you are drinking you could be spending upwards of $100 on that as well. That is

$3,000 a year that you can put toward something more important. Saving money and being frugal has a lot to do with being healthy as well and just imagine the amount of money you will end up saving on future doctor bills if you quit now.

9. Shop at thrift shops and yard sales. You may think that you will not find anything that you like if you purchase from thrift shops or yard sales, but the truth is you can find amazing treasures. For example, my entire living room is furnished with Ashley furniture. I bought it at a yard sale from an elderly couple. It was very well cared for and I spent a total of $200 for a couch, loveseat, and two chairs. All of the pictures in my home have come from thrift shops, as well as all of the televisions I own. You can purchase a 40-inch television from a thrift shop for about $40. This is because they usually do not have the remote with them, but guess what; you can order a universal remote from Amazon for about $10. So you end up spending around $50 for the entire thing!

10. Find things to do that do not cost any money. Often times people get bored and they decide that they want to go spend some money to entertain themselves, instead find things to do that are free. Such as a hike in the woods, visiting your local park, taking your kids swimming in the river or teaching them about volunteering at the local animal shelter. You can also watch your local paper for free events that are being held in your town such as parades, car shows or cook offs.

# Chapter 4

# And There is More!

There are even more ways for you to save money each and every day! I know at this point you may be getting a little overwhelmed, but choose a few money saving ideas from this book and implement them. Once you are able to do them with consistency add a few more. This is not all or nothing here. Remember, saving just a little will help you become encouraged to save even more!

1. Take advantage of end of season sales. Did you know that you can get brand name clothes brand new for literally pennies on the dollar? At the end of each season clothing goes on sale, if you watch the prices you will be able to get $100 shirts for a couple bucks! When you have growing kids this is a great way to keep them in stylish clothing without breaking the bank. What I do is purchase one or two sizes bigger than what my child is currently wearing so that the new clothes will fit when that season comes around again. You can also do this for holiday decorations, costumes, and even purchase your Christmas presents for the next year right after this years Christmas! You will end up saving about 90% on Christmas and you will be prepared for the following year!

2. Cook all of your meals at home. If you find that you are going out to eat more than once a month, you really need to think about cooking more meals at home. You see, for what you spend on one meal at a fast food place,

you could make dinner for four at home and it's going to be much more healthy.

3. If something is broken, do not throw it away, fix it! We live in a society where everything is disposable, but if you really want to save money, learn how to fix the things that are broken.

4. Rent instead of own. There are those who will disagree with this, but if you rent a house instead of purchase it, you don't have to pay home owners insurance, you don't have to worry about how you will pay for a new water heater, just call the landlord and let them deal with it.

5. Move to a smaller cheaper house. This is one that gets a lot of people. We want our children to have their own bedrooms, to have a huge house to live in and we want others to think we are well off. If you are paying for more house than you really need, you are wasting your money. I had to consider this when I was living in a five bedroom house realizing we actually only used a few of the rooms. So much space was not being used, therefore so much of my money was being wasted. Look into a smaller cheaper house if you find that all of your house is not being used.

6. Plant a garden. Gardening is very inexpensive and it can produce lots of great food for you to eat. You can also sell the excess at your local farmers market in order to make some extra cash on the side!

7. Raise your own chickens. Many people have trouble eating the chickens that they raise, so for those people, just get enough chickens to produce the number of eggs you need each day! If you have extra sell them. In the summer, you can allow your chickens to roam your yard and eat up all the bugs along with some grass to cut back on chicken feed.

8. Learn how to cut your own hair or at least your children's hair. In our house, I cut everyone's hair except my own. I have very long hair and when I want it trimmed I am willing to pay the $8 to have it done, but only once or twice a year. If you can cut your own hair that is great, if not find a low priced salon and have them do it on the cheap.

9. Dying your own hair can also save you a ton of money. With salon prices sky rocketing, you can save about $100 each time you dye your hair at home depending on how long it is.

10. Take snacks with you wherever you go. How often do you jump in the car to go somewhere and the kids start complaining that they are hungry? You end up stopping by a fast food joint and spending $40 on junk food. Instead, grab some Ziploc bags and stuff them full of healthy snacks. The next time the kids say they are, hungry hand them a bag and be on your way.

# Chapter 5

# Final Tips for You to Save Money!

In this next chapter, I am going to give you ten more tips to help you save money. Here are ten more tips to help save you money every day!

1. Find out if your bank is charging you fees. What happens if your bank account gets overdrawn by accident? How much do you end up paying? If you find that you are paying fees at your bank, find a bank that works for you. For example, my bank offers a plan for free that allows you to overdraw by $600 as long as you pay off the balance within a month. This is great in case there is some type of emergency and you don't have to worry about paying $30 a day in overdraft fees!

2. Have your bills automatically taken out of your bank account each month. Life is fast and sometimes we forget to send that bill or jump online to pay it, so instead of getting charged late fees each month, just sign up to auto pay your bills each month. This can save a few hundred dollars in late fees each year.

3. Sell the things you don't need! Don't give away the clothes that your children have out grown, take them to a thrift shop and sell them on consignment or better yet have a yard sale and make some extra cash. I always

send everything to the thrift shop because I don't have much time to plan a yard sale and they do all the work for me. You do need to understand they will take a percentage of what your stuff sells for though.

4. Stop buying paper towels (unless of course you have a coupon that makes them free). Instead of buying paper towels, go buy a pack of white wash cloths for $3 that you will use specifically for cleaning.

5. Freeze the items you buy in bulk. A few weeks ago I went to the local discount grocery store and they had Coffee Mate creamer on sale for 2 for a dollar. This stuff is very expensive, so I purchased several. I knew that if I did not use them quickly they would go bad, so instead, I put them in the freezer and each week I can grab one out to use. I now have enough creamer for several months and saved around $80! You can freeze tons of items you find on sale like this, and if you don't know ask someone who works at the store, they can usually tell you.

6. If you are going to run your appliances (dishwasher, washing machine, dryer) run them at night. The off peak hour prices for electricity are cheaper than during the day!

7. Save all of your change for a year. Each time you empty your pockets or your purse, put your loose change in a jar, at the end of the year deposit this change into a savings account.

8. Do you get a tax return? Many people with children get a tax return each year, many of these people also end up wasting this money on items they do not really need. Instead of wasting your tax return, create a plan to use it to pay up your bills for several months in advance, or use it to pay down some of that debt. This is a great chance for you to benefit yourself in the days to come.

9. Use a thirty-day plan. If you are in the store and you see something that you want, put it back on the shelf and wait for thirty days. If in thirty days you still want the item, see if you can fit it into your budget, but chances are you are going to forget about the item because you only wanted it on impulse.

10. Need it or want it. Many people have to realize there is a difference between need and want. They go into the store see an item they want and tell themselves they need it for this specific reason. A need is something that you will not be able to live without. A want is obviously something you can live without but would really like. Ask yourself if you really need the item before buying it.

# Chapter 6

# How to Get Out of Debt for Good

Throughout this book, I have given you tips on how to save money, but what are you supposed to do with the money you are saving? Of course you can put it in the bank in a savings account, but before you do that you want to get yourself out of debt.

It does not matter what kind of debt you have, the technique I am going to teach you will get you completely out of debt in the shortest amount of time possible.

First, I want you to get a pen and paper and start writing down all of the debt you own and how much you currently own on that debt. Like this:

| | |
|---|---|
| Medical | $6,543 |
| MasterCard | $4,154 |
| Visa | $2,894 |
| Car | $7,325 |

And so on. Now once you have your list, you are going to find the debt that you owe the least amount on. Using the above example, you would want to begin with the Visa card. If your minimum monthly payment is $200, I want you to budget that $200 into your monthly bills. I also want you to add an extra $50 to $100 onto the payment depending on how much you can afford.

Keep making your minimum payments on the rest of your bills until the Visa is paid in full. Next, you would move on to the MasterCard. Let's say you have been paying $300 a month toward that debt, I want you to take that $300 plus the $200 you were paying for your Visa as well as the $50 to $100 dollars you added on to the minimum payment and pay that all towards your MasterCard. This would make your payment $550 to $600 dollars a month.

After you have paid off your MasterCard, you are going to move on to the next bill. In this example you would begin paying off your medical bills. So, if you are paying a minimum of $100 dollars per month toward your medical bills, you are going to take the $200 you were paying toward your Visa before it was paid off, plus the $50 to $100 extra you were sending in, add to that the $300 you were paying toward your MasterCard before it was paid off, and you will be sending $650-$700 dollars per month toward your medical bills.

You will continue this process until all of your debt is paid off. Then, you will keep following the tips I have given you in this book to ensure you do not accrue more debt. It is important that you take the money you were paying toward previous bills and budget it for the next bill, because otherwise you are going to find yourself spending and wasting all of that money that should be going to bills. Once your debt is paid off, you need to set it up with your bank so the money is deposited directly into a savings account each and every month.

Doing this will ensure that you are not wasting your money, but setting up a nice nest egg for yourself and your family.

This process is simple, but depending on the amount of debt, you have it can take some time. Remember the tip I gave you about your tax return, if you do get one, you can also use this to pay down these debts making the process go much, much faster.

# Chapter 7

# Frugal Lifestyle

Living frugally and without debt is a lifestyle and it may take some time for you to get used to it, but it is so freeing that it is worth all of the work that goes into it. When you decide that you want to live frugally and without debt, sit down and make a list of reasons why you want to do so.

Keep this list of reasons close by so that if you start to feel like you are missing out on certain things in life you will be reminded of what your goals are. One of the rules in our house is that if we don't have a coupon for it, we do not purchase it. So, if you really are wanting something search the internet for a coupon for it or just wait until it goes on sale.

Another part of living the frugal lifestyle is taking care of the things you have and respecting what you have spent your money on. So what if you own a $50 couch, that is $50 out of your pocket, take care of it and respect it.

Finally, I want to talk to you about passing on the frugal lifestyle. How great would it feel if you could say your children would never be in debt? What about if you knew that they would never go without or want because you taught them how to save and spend money wisely. If for no other reason than this, I hope that you take the tips in this book and implement them into your life.

You must understand before you decide to make these changes, that living frugally and saving money does take some extra work in life! It does take giving up some conveniences, but trust me if you follow through with this in a few months you won't even miss them.

Now, how are you going to implement these changes? As I mentioned before, I want you to pick a few of the tips I have given you and start making those changes in your life. Once you have applied these changes, after a few weeks add a few more changes.

You don't want to make too many changes at once because if you do you will find that they are harder to stick to. Most people want to make huge changes in their lives and they fail because they really are asking too much of themselves. But if you add in small changes, you will barely notice them and you will raise your chances of being successful.

One thing that you are going to do while you are making these changes is fail. You are going to see something in the store that you really like and buy it on impulse or order something off of the internet, but when this happens don't give up, keep your head up and start again.

We as humans only learn through failure and if you fail along the way, take note of it then move on. This only gets easier as time goes on.

# Conclusion

I hope this book was able to help you to save money, get out of debt and live a more frugal life!

The next step is to get started using these tips and paying off that debt!

Finally, if you enjoyed this book, then I'd like to ask you for a favor, would you be kind enough to leave a review for this book on Amazon? It'd be greatly appreciated!

# LIVING FRUGAL
## And *Loving It*

### 40 CREATIVE WAYS TO SAVE MONEY AND LIVE DEBT FREE FOR LIFE

KATHY STANTON

# Introduction

This book contains proven steps and strategies on how you can spend less and save more, by making simple, easy to follow changes in your day-to-day life.

While many people think that living frugally means you have to deny yourself the things you love, this doesn't have to be the case. Instead, be realistic about what you can do, and find small, practical ways to create big changes! In this definitive guide, we've listed 40 tips and tricks that will benefit you on your path to frugal living, ultimately helping you gain the financial freedom you desire.

Thanks again for purchasing this book, I hope you enjoy it!

# Chapter 1: Looking at the Big Picture

With the cost of living increasing every year, there is no better time than the present to take a look at your day-to-day life, and find places where you could be saving money and reducing waste. Below are some simple tips that will help get you started.

1. **Use less**
   While this may seem like common sense, many of us would be shocked to realize how much we waste daily, in almost every facet of our lives. Most of us could afford to use less in numerous areas including: food, beauty products, gas, clothing, natural resources, and other consumables. Think about enacting small changes like trying to use less toothpaste when you brush, or ensuring that you use only enough laundry detergent to wash the load size you have. For many of us our impulse seems to be more is better, and we don't even try to limit ourselves when we should. Try to be conscious of your consumption and your costs will reduce.
2. **List your goals**
   It can prove very helpful if you jot down a list of your long-term priorities, such as saving for a house, or remodeling a current home. When you have set financial goals you are working toward, it is much easier to remain focused on saving money to achieve

that goal. Try to make sure that your savings are only going toward these further out goals, and not being spent on short-tem goals such as vacations. If you have short-term goals you'd like to achieve, try to draw the money from other areas of your budget, such as entertainment or eating out.

3. **Plan ahead**

    While this is easy enough to say, it can often prove much more difficult to implement. If you make it a habit to think far in advance about what is going on in your life, you will ultimately save a significant amount of money. For example, if you know that you will be traveling, make sure to pack a dinner or a lunch. If you find yourself unprepared you'll likely eat your meal at a restaurant (at an increased cost). If you know that you'll be out all day, grab a reusable bottle of water to avoid paying significantly more if you have to purchase it. Is there an important birthday coming up? Grab a gift on sale in advance instead of scrambling the day of for an appropriate present.

4. **Look in advance for significant purchases**

    It is always in your best interest to look in advance, and do your research, before making any decisions on a significant purchase. For big expenditures like appliances or vehicles, keep your eyes peeled for sales, and don't be in a rush. Have a clear idea of what you want, and what a general cost might be both new and used. Often if you have patience, and a strong knowledge of what something is worth, a deal may present itself.

5. **Never buy things full price**

While this is a rule you can't always stick to, it is one that you should always aim for if at all possible. If you need something take the time to research the standard price and possible sale prices, as well as any discounts or coupons that may apply. Consider also your buying options such as online or in store. Try to buy things like clothing in the off-season when items are likely to be reduced to sell. Keep in mind that many retailers will have a price-match policy, so knowing your stuff will ensure that you can take full advantage of this option.

6. **Re-evaluate your transportation**

    One of the more significant costs that a household can incur is that of owning and operating a vehicle. Between car payments, gas, insurance, and general maintenance, your car can often be a serious financial drain. Why not try riding your bike, walking, or if your city has it, making use of public transit? If you need a car you can always rent one, and you'll probably still save thousands of dollars a year. If saying goodbye to your car is not an option for you, explore the idea of carpooling. Carpooling allows multiple people to share the cost of gas, parking, and other car-related incidentals that can often add up.

7. **Hand make your gifts**

    While not everyone is an artist, with the proliferation of DIY online tutorials, and the social networking site Pinterest, almost anyone can whip up a creative and thoughtful gift. Taking the time to make a gift for someone not only shows a level of care that they will appreciate, it will often end up saving you a significant amount of money.

8. **Consider used first**
   While it can be tempting to own something shiny and new, used is always a good option to explore. When you are looking for a specific item, put out feelers to see if anyone you know, or any of their connections, are selling something similar. Ask around, send out an email, or post your request on a community board (either online or in high traffic areas where you live). You'll be surprised how often what you need it out there, and by reaching out, you are giving someone else a chance to get rid of something they may no longer want, while still getting what you need. If none of your direct contacts have what you are looking for, you can always check online sites such as Craigslist or Freecycle, to see if there are any possible bargains there. A great way to do this is to have a running list of items that you are looking for, so that you are not just focusing on one. Refer back to these sites often to see if there are any new items that catch your eye. If it is not on your list, don't buy it! These sites should be used to make you more frugal, not lead to you buying more stuff.

9. **Focus on increasing your income**
   While online sites such as Craigslist or eBay can be great resources when you are looking to purchase items, they can also bring you extra income. Post items you no longer want that may have value to someone else. You can often make a little money on things you would otherwise just get rid of. Also, try exploring whether you can pick up extra cash by doing freelance or contract work. Websites like oDesk and Elance will put you in contact with clients who need work done on a per

job basis, which allows you to fit it into your schedule. Take any extra income you make this way and ensure that you put it directly into savings, so that it doesn't get eaten up but non-essential costs.

# Chapter 2: Eating & Entertaining on a Budget

From entertaining at home, to reducing your food bill, there are many ways to limit your costs that don't have to mean sacrificing the things you love. Look no further than your kitchen when you are searching for ways to save.

10. **Eat out less**
    One of the largest, most unnecessary daily expenditures that people make, is eating outside of the home. The average person wastes over $2,000 a year visiting fast-food chains and dining in restaurants. This can be expensive, never mind bad for your health (which can also have long term effects on your spending if you become ill). It is always cheaper to prepare you own food. Try creating a weekly menu and sticking to it. It is important that eating out becomes the exception, and not the rule in your household. If you do have to eat at a restaurant, try a few tips that will make sure your bill doesn't break the bank. Skip the alcohol or soft drinks, and instead ask for water. Water will fill you up and cause you to consume less, while also being free! Perhaps consider splitting a meal with someone, as most places offer ridiculous, unnecessary portions. You'll be looking after your health, and your wallet, and if you feel silly doing it, you've saved enough money to lessen your embarrassment by giving the server a great tip.
11. **Cut coupons and search for vouchers**
    Coupons and vouchers are a valuable tool in a frugal

person's arsenal. Check weekly flyers, clip coupons when you see them, and search online for codes and vouchers. Deals will be offered in almost every area that you spend in, so keep your eyes peeled! Know however, that while coupons and vouchers can save you money, it only works if you purchase things that you normally would. Don't clip coupons for luxury items that you wouldn't usually buy. Coupons should assist you with the necessities, not add another shopping item to your list.

12. **Brown paper bag your lunches**

    Absolutely everyone has the ability to plan ahead and pack a lunch, and anyone who uses time constraints as an excuse isn't using their money saving smarts. A packed or prepared lunch will often cost less than $3, and take you only a few minutes to throw together. In comparison, eating out or grabbing something quickly, will more likely fall in the $7 - $20 range. This is one area where people are constantly careless, thoughtlessly cutting into their money saving potential by make hasty eating decisions.

13. **Cook ahead of time**

    For many people cooking a week or even a month in advance can be an amazing way to save money. Plan a free day where you can cook food in large batches and then freeze them in dinner-sized potions. While this isn't something that people can do all the time, it can save money if utilized even occasionally. There is a fair amount of planning involved in this, but once completed it will remove the day-to-day meal planning that often poses an issue for overworked and exhausted people. Often when we are tired we revert to eating out or grabbing convenience foods, and having easy, available options at home will at least curb that tendency.

14. **Get a deep freeze**
Investing in a large freezer can be a great way to save yourself some money down the line. Lots of space will ensure that you can preplan your meals in advance, as well as buy perishable items in bulk. Try stocking up on certain foods when they are on sale, and keep them in the deep freeze until you need them. Reduced cuts of meat, homemade bread, and fresh fruits and vegetables bought when in season, can all be safely stored in the freezer for future use. Knowing that you have a full freezer of available options can also be a comfort to people during times when money isn't quite as plentiful.

15. **Search out affordable recipes**
There are numerous online sites, as well as specialized cookbooks, that will provide you with affordable, nutritious recipe options. Especially if you are a newbie in the kitchen (but even if you are not), these sites and books can prove invaluable. These sources will often inform you on a variety of topics including the best, most affordable cuts of meat to use in recipes, as well as what is in season (and often priced lower) at certain times of the year. Recipes may also offer a general cost per portion, which can be helpful information for people trying to make better financial choices.

16. **Grow and make your own food**
Growing your own garden can be an amazing way to cut

costs in the kitchen. Think of the vegetables and herbs that you use most, and plant them in the spring, to reap the benefits in the summer. A garden can yield a significant amount of food, and an overabundance of it can always be frozen or canned for later use. Explore also making your own versions of food you can purchase in the store. Make your own bread, try dehydrating fruit, or look up recipes for fresh homemade versions of food you can buy premade, such as hummus or guacamole.

17. **Buy in bulk**

    While many sales and buy-one-get-one-free offers are designed to convince you to buy things you normally wouldn't, there are usually a few items worth grabbing at a reduced price. Be on the lookout for sales and specials on non-perishable items that you frequently need such as canned goods, pasta, and rice. These are items that you know you will eventually use, so if you can find a good deal stock up. Only buy in bulk for these types of necessities or you could end up with items you don't want or need.

18. **Have a concept of the average prices for common goods**

    Being prepared and doing your homework is a major component of staying thrifty when you are grocery shopping. Do a little detective work before you head out and compare the cost of food staples at different stores available to you. See if you can deduce any trends in the items that are usually more affordable at each store. You may end up having multiple grocery stores that each offer something that you want. For example one may be generally the most affordable, while another may have the best prices for meat or produce. Try to organize you grocery shopping to ensure that you are getting what you need from each store. If you don't have a solid concept of what an average price is, you leave yourself susceptible to purchases that may be significantly more than you would have paid elsewhere.

19. **Make your own alcohol**

    If you entertain regularly, or if you enjoy a glass of wine or a cold beer, it can often be very cost efficient for you to look into making your own alcohol. While there is some cost for set-up if you are making it out of your own house, it will quickly be absorbed when you realize you are stocking your wine cellar and beer fridge for a fraction of what you would pay in stores. If you like the price point but aren't willing to do all the work, there are many make your own wine and beer facilities that will help you with the process, while still offering a significantly lower cost per bottle.

20. **Entertain your friends at home**

    Are you a social butterfly who loves spending quality time with your friends, but doesn't necessarily have the budget for dinner and drinks on the town? Why not trying hosting a night-in at your place, where people can each bring a different snack or potluck dish, and you can organize games or a movie viewing? This may require a little more planning than a trip to a restaurant, but your wallet will reap the benefits. Keep in mind that if you are planning a party where an invitation is required, you can use online services like Evite to take advantage of free, or low-cost options. If you need supplies such as napkins, cups, or plates, stock up when you see them on sale, or hit up your local dollar store. Spending time with your friends doesn't have to mean spending tons of cash.

21. **Drink more water**.

    This one seems simple because it is. Water is refreshing and hydrating, and even more importantly to the frugal – it's free! Cut out alcohol, soft drinks, coffee, tea and juices, and you'll find immediately that you have a little extra cash in your pocket.

# Chapter 3: Health & Beauty Hacks to Save Money

While keeping ourselves looking and feeling good is important, there are ways that we can ensure that we are still being financially conscious, and watching our consumption. While you don't have to scrimp, here are a few helpful hints on how to save a little cash while still taking care of yourself.

22. **Don't buy name brand over the counter medication**

    For many common medications such as pain relievers or anti-histamines, the ingredients are virtually identical when you compare name brand and generic. Check bulk stores for large bottles of the medications you use, and when there is a choice, opt for the house brand. There is absolutely no difference in how they will work. Also, try searching online for a greater choice of generic brands that may be even more affordable. Often you can score a great deal just by shopping around and checking your options.

23. **Ditch the gym**

    For many people a gym membership is something they underutilize at the best of times, while for others it is a complete waste of money. Regardless of whether you make use of a membership or not, know that there are many other options for keeping fit that you can explore for a fraction of the cost of the gym. Walk, run, cycle, or just get outside! If you'd rather stick close to home, look into the numerous online resources that offer free yoga, fitness, and dance classes (among other options). There are ways to keep fit that don't have to break the bank. Remember though, while we don't advise you shell out a ton of money on the gym, keep in mind that maintaining your physical fitness is an investment you should make. When you focus on preventative care you are ensuring a future not bogged down by poor health and the financial issues that often accompany it.

24. **Good to the last drop**

    While many of us like to pretend that we are super conscious about wasting our resources, we often act quite carelessly with things that cost us money. We may casually toss a not quite empty toothpaste because we can't get it from the bottom of the tube, or throw out a moisturizer because it doesn't come out with quite the same quantity as before. In order to be thrifty it is important to ensure that we are using everything to the last drop. We can do this by cutting up tubes and emptying them completely before we throw them away.

# Chapter 4: Checking Your Financial Fitness

Being financially in the know can be liberating, and having a solid grasp on where to cut, and where to save, can really help you on your path to financial freedom. Keep a close eye on your funds and make use of the tips below.

25. **Bank smarter**
    Banking smarter means making any number of small changes that will increase the amount of money that you are saving. A great way to get started is by switching your bank account over to a provider who offers no-fee accounts. There is no reason you should be paying maintenance or usage fees, so find someone who will offer you an alternative. Try also to see if you can negotiate credit card or loan interest rates with you bank. It never hurts to ask, and often you will receive! Banking is a competitive business, so if they can't offer you a deal that makes you happy, look elsewhere. Keep in mind though, that one surefire way to save yourself money is by reducing any unnecessary credit you may be paying interest on. Have a credit card if it is absolutely necessary, but keep the balance low, or pay it off monthly to ensure that you aren't wasting dollars that could be going elsewhere.
26. **Have an automatic savings plan**
    A great way to start flexing your frugality muscles is by

transferring money automatically off of your paychecks. Put this money directly into a savings account, and consider it not part of the money you can spend. We tend to try to live to whatever means we have, so often bigger paychecks just means more spending. Remove the extra cash from the equation and see what you can make due with. 20% is a great starting point, but evaluate how that works for you and increase or decrease accordingly. If you don't see the money, chances are you won't miss it. The only stipulation to this rule is if you are carrying significant debt. If this is the case only have a small emergency savings fund, as you want to be allocating money to debt, which is a serious money drain that you should try to remove.

27. **Use a rewards credit card**

    While the truly frugal would advocate for no credit, rewards credit cards can be a great option for those who have a solid handle on their spending. Often new cards will offer sign-up bonuses in cash, air miles, or points. If you can take advantage of these responsibly, and not increase your consumption at all, this can be a great benefit. This is essentially extra money that you wouldn't have had otherwise. Using your rewards cards to pay for everything, including bills, will help you amass benefits that you wouldn't with a debit card. This can only work if you spend responsibly though.
    Running up a credit card to get air miles doesn't work if you are spending hundreds every month in interest.

# Chapter 5: Targeting the Technology Cash Drain

We live in a world dominated by technology, and for many of us it is an absolute necessity. Take some time however to consider if there are any technological conveniences you can cut or reduce to save yourself some dollars.

28. **Limit your devices**

    While it can be fun to have all the new gadgets that litter the market, try to really consider what you need technology wise. If your job requires you to write briefs or create complex presentations, then a laptop may be necessary. If however, you end up using your laptop purely to surf the net or check emails, you might consider just having a smart phone that does everything you need at a reduced cost. Many people also have cross over in the devices that they own, owning multiple items that do the same things. One person doesn't need an IPod, IPhone, IPad and Mac computer, but it is very likely that many people possess all of these things. Try to really evaluate your needs and downsize when not necessary.

29. **Cut your cable**

    Gone are the days when cable television connected you to everything that was happening in the world. With the advent of online sites where you can view virtually anything you want, and the arrival of very low cost subscription packages, cable is no longer a necessity for many households. Save some cash by downsizing or removing an expensive package, and pick and choose what you want from affordable online options. Often cable leads to endless channel surfing, and killing time watching things you aren't really interested in. A positive side effect of ditching it is that you may only end up watching television for specific programs, leading to less time wasted on the couch.

**30.     Negotiate with your providers**

Many companies that provide services like phone and internet service, can afford to be more flexible than they would have you believe. Just because they present you with a price, doesn't mean that is the final offer. Don't be afraid to call customer service and let them know that you are exploring other options. Check in with them every few months and see what new deals they are offering to new clients. Once they've already secured your business they certainly won't be calling you to reduce your bill, but if they can offer to new people, they should be able to offer it to you. It never hurts to ask, and often you can secure some great deals.

# Chapter 6: Don't be House Poor

Your home is your palace, and for many of us (especially those trying to cut back on costs) it is where we spend the majority of our time. Ensure that your home isn't a drain on your finances by following the tips below.

31. **Get the house you NEED, not the house you WANT**

    In the competitive housing market banks often try to offer incredibly low interest rates and high mortgage approvals to entice buyers. Just because you are approved for a $500,000 mortgage, doesn't mean you have to take it. Think seriously about what type of house possesses all of the things you need, without veering too far into what you want on top of that. You may be able to find a house for $200,000 that fits all of your criteria, so don't be tempted by the more expensive house. While it may be nicer, if the other house fits your conditions, there is no logical reason to pay more. Keep in mind that you may think you can afford a larger mortgage, but when you factor in utilities, property taxes, upkeep, and unexpected incidentals that will arise, you may be in for more than you bargained for.

32. **Ensure the efficiency of your home**

    Your home can often be one of the major money drains in your life. While some things are beyond your control, there are a few things you can do to ensure that your house isn't siphoning money directly from your savings. First, ensure that it is properly insulated. This can include checking for any places that heat might escape from, and windows are often a key culprit. Make sure that windows are not a heat drain, and replace anything that threatens to hike up your bills. If you can't afford to replace windows you can cover them with plastic in the cooler months to keep warm air from escaping and cooler air getting in. Also, ensure that you are using appliances and electricity wisely. Turn off lights when you leave a room, and try not to use water for laundry or dishwashing during peak hours. Finally, try not to fiddle too much with your thermostat. Even moving it by a few degrees can seriously affect your utility bills. Throw on a sweater or invest in a pair of slippers, and your bank account will thank you.

### 33. Make your own cleaning products

While supermarket cleaning products can often cost a premium, a quick look in your cupboards may offer you a multitude of ingredients that can also do the trick, at a fraction of the price. Try using a teaspoon of bicarbonate of soda on a damp cloth to mimic a cream cleanser. White vinegar is also an amazing all-purpose ingredient whether you are washing your windows or cleaning your floors. There is absolutely no reason to pay high prices for brand-name items when you can do a quick search on the internet that will reveal numerous cleaning product recipes that will save you money, and keep your house spotless.

### 34. Master the art of DIY

While there are some things, like plumbing and electrical, which should be left to professionals, there are a lot of do-it-yourself tricks that you can employ to save yourself some money. Online tutorials in how to do small repairs around your home make undertaking household projects that much easier. You can also visit your larger hardware stores for information on projects like tiling and painting. When you fix something yourself, you not only gain a serious sense of accomplishment, you also save money!

# Chapter 7: Looking Good For Less

While it can be fun to have new clothes, this is a major area of expenditure for a lot of people, and one of the most obvious places that you can make changes for the better. Consider these tips below before buying new, or tossing the old.

### 35. Wash clothes less

While some people wear clothes once and then throw them in the wash, this isn't necessarily the best way to maintain the colour and quality of your items. Unless you have a job which involves your clothes getting extremely dirty, or you hit the gym and sweat profusely, most clothes can be worn more than once before tossing them in the wash. Use the smell test to deduce whether they are actually dirty or not. You'll know right away if they can stick around for another wear, or if it is time to put them in the hamper. This can save you money on washing, but it will also serve to extend the life of your clothing.

### 36. Hang-dry clothes

While dryers are fast, they aren't always the best option if you are looking to curb energy usage and prolong the life of your clothing. Especially if you are doing smaller loads, take a few minutes to hang them up. If the sun is shining they'll be dry before you know it, but even drying on racks inside can be better for your items and save your electricity bills. Air-drying means that nothing is being shrunk or damaged, and this can save you even more money in the long run when you don't have to buy new clothes.

### 37. Shop at consignment boutiques

Clothing shopping is another area where you can opt to buy used. Visit consignment shops where you can often find high-quality items at a seriously reduced price. In fact, many items will be barely used, and if you have patience you should be able to land yourself a few great pieces. When shopping vintage you can also raid your parents' or grandparents' old closets for pieces from previous decades. You can hit on some really beautiful items that may be the height of fashion this way. Don't let snobbery or distaste for second-hand, stop you from finding amazing bargains.

## 38. Spend money on quality

While it often seems counterintuitive when you are trying to be frugal, it is often wise to pay more money for clothing than less. Often cheaper items are low quality and won't be able to hold out long enough for you to refresh them or prolong their life. High quality items may come with a higher price tag, but try to think of them as investments. Buy staples that you can wear for years, instead of disposable clothing that won't last a season. Evaluate the quality of clothing by checking the stitching for loose threads, and ensure that any patterns match up. Try also bunching the material in your hand for a few seconds and then watch if it returns to its natural shape. Make smart fashion choices and you should have high-quality items for more than long enough to justify the cost.

## 39. Take care of your clothes

While day-to-day wear and tear is unavoidable, you can often prolong the life of your clothing with a few simple steps. Instead of throwing away fuzzy sweaters use a razor blade to remove pilling and refresh the wool. Try also dying faded jeans, or digging out the sewing machine to repair any clothing with missing buttons or small holes. If you are bored of what is in your closet, try to get creative by bringing new life to old items. Head to markets or sewing shops and find artistic supplies to jazz up tired old apparel. Check fashion magazines and internet images for inspiration, and make it your own!

40. **Host a clothing swap**

A clothing swap can be a great way to get rid of items you no longer want, while acquiring new ones at no cost! Ask your girlfriends to go through their closets and bring items they want to get rid of. Have them bring everything to a get-together where everyone gets to sort through and pick out the items they like. Throw in some appetizers and wine and you've got a party! This idea can also be extended to include children's clothing, if you have a group of mothers with kids of differing ages.

# Conclusion

Thank you again for downloading this book!

I hope this book was able to help inspire you to immediately start looking at the ways in which you can limit consumption, and save money in your daily life.

The next step is to cultivate a conscious awareness of the ways in which you can make use of the tips and tricks in this book, ensuring yourself the financial freedom and security you desire.

Thank you and good luck!

# Introduction

This book contains proven steps and strategies on how to minimize your "stuff" in order to live a clutter-free and enjoyable life. We have all done it. Looking around our home or office, we see the stuff that we wish we could hide. We have visions of a showroom home that is clean and tidy. However, that doesn't follow through into our lives.

 Our lives are full of clutter and it can be a huge eyesore to both you and those who visit you. Why do you put up with it? If you're ready for a change, then try some of the creative ways that I will talk about in this book to make your space seem uncluttered and simple. You can have a room that mirrors a showroom with just a few simple changes to your life.

# Chapter 1- Clutter vs. Necessity

Let's get real here. In a world where quantity definitely overrides quality, people obtain more and more stuff that just ends up piling up. You might find a few good things in your piles, but for the most part, you can probably live without most of the items sitting in front of you at this very moment. All of that stuff that you felt you needed to have is unused and wasted money. Have you ever thought about how you can maintain a simple life and not have so much stuff?

You are not the only one who faces this struggle. With many like you, you have a support system that can help you get past the clutter stage and into the open-feeling stage. It takes time, and it takes patience, but if you are determined to weed out your unwanted and unnecessary belongings, you will find that your home or office will feel more open and free.

However, there is one battle that you have to overcome. What do you own that would be considered clutter and what would be considered necessity? By asking yourself whether or not you really use or need a certain object will help you begin to shed yourself of all the items that just aren't a part of your life. Understanding that they are just things will also help you in the battle to part with items that you might like but don't need.

Take a look around the room that you are sitting in right now. You can probably spot at least a half dozen items that you can easily give away and never miss. Why do you still have them? What is the point in keeping them? Some people tell themselves that they will eventually use them, but eventually doesn't always come. If you are in that mindset, then just save yourself the trouble of planning on using it and get rid of it! This will take care of one piece of clutter in your life!

Once you can differentiate clutter from necessity, you can begin the process of uncluttering your home and making it possible to feel as though you have space to move about. This can be a liberating for you. No one realizes just how much getting rid of unnecessary stuff can really feel! Also, when you have less, it becomes easier to maintain your home, and it also gives you the time and ability to spend time with others. It's a winning situation all around, so why not go for it?

If you feel doubts about parting with items in your life, think about others who could really use what you don't use. By giving your possessions away, you're not only simplifying your life, but you are helping those who need what you have. If you don't use it, and you will never look at it again, then don't be selfish and keep it. You're not only hurting yourself, but you are also hurting someone who can use what you are keeping to yourself.

So, if you're ready to make the change and want to know how you can make these changes, keep on reading! I will provide you with creative ways to declutter your home and simplify your life!

# Chapter 2- Tips to Decluttering and Simplifying Your Living Space

Your main living space is what your friends, family and any other visitor that comes around will notice first. Sadly enough, people will judge you by what your home looks like. Seeing that your main living space feels cluttered might give them the wrong impression of you as a person. So, let's focus on how to declutter your living space and making it feel more open and inviting to your visitors.

Picture in your mind what you would like your living space to look like. What can you do to make sure that it look like it does in your mind? Try putting together a list of what will need to be done in order to achieve the picture that you have in your mind.

*Getting Rid of the Junk*

One of the most time-consuming but most necessary elements of simplifying and decluttering is getting rid of unnecessary items in your home. Deciding on what to get rid of and what to keep can take a lot of time and energy. This can be especially true if you're a person who may place sentimental value in objects. However, we must learn to separate that item from the memory and part with items that are no longer needed or used.

After you have parted with your junk, then you can effectively begin organizing and simplifying your home with what you have left.

*Downsizing Furniture*

Large furniture can easily take up space and make your home look small and cluttered. Try finding pieces that suit your home and your room sizes. This will allow your room to feel larger and more open. If you live alone, there really is no reason for you to have a full living room set when a chair or a small loveseat would suit you perfectly. Think about the implications your furniture might have on the feel of your home and consider downsizing in order to make your space feel larger.

*Arrange Your Furniture in an Inviting Way*

If you have too much furniture or not enough space, try rearranging your furniture so that it helps your room feel more inviting and more open. A lot of furniture can be used as room dividers and shelves can be set up behind sofas to create a homey look. Take the furniture you currently have and try arranging it in different ways that make your room feel simple and inviting. It might take a couple of tries, but once you find the arrangement you like, then you will have a living room that will be suitable for guests.

*Keep the Décor Simple*

One of the most crucial ways to simplify your home is to cut back on your decorations. I will cover this a bit more later on, but having to many decorations will make a room feel full and cluttered, even if the room is large and there is nothing else to make it feel cluttered. Try limiting what you have on your walls, mantle and shelves. Keeping it simple will help it become much more roomy and inviting.

*Tone Down the Colors*

Bold and dark colors can easily make your room look dark or overwhelming. Try using earthy and light colors. This tip works for both your decorations and for your furniture. The lighter it looks, the more open and airy your room will feel. If you don't like extremely light colors, try medium tones that won't overpower the room and make it feel small. Try looking in decorating magazines and find rooms that appeal to you and try to imitate their decorating style in your own home.

*Make Sure it Has Enough Lighting*

Sometimes, the rooms in your home will not receive a whole lot of natural lighting. This can make the room feel dark and dreary, even if you have light colored décor. If you have a room like this in your home, try using lamps and other forms of lighting to make the room feel brighter and happier. You can buy many different types of lamps that can light your room and give you the feel that you wish to achieve. Even a dim room can feel cozy if it is lit in the right way.

*Have Enough Open Floor Space*

If you cannot walk through a room, then you know that you have a problem with clutter. Floor space is important in making your home feel open and simple. If you find that you have too much furniture, then it might be time to consider getting rid of some of it and making your room feel larger. No one wants to dodge furniture with every step in order to make it through that room, and it could lead to accidents in the middle of the night.

Starting my decluttering and organizing your living space can help you to get a feel for what you would like the rest of your home to look like. This might be the largest part of your project, but once your main room feels open and simple, you will get the motivation to continue to work through the rest of your home. Simple doesn't always mean that you go minimalist, it just means that you are making your home feel less cluttered and more inviting. Cutting back on what you have in your living area, whether it be dark colors or too much furniture, can lead to your entire home feeling simpler.

# Chapter 3- Tips for Decluttering and Simplifying Your Personal Space

When looking at your personal space, such as your bathroom or bedroom, it might feel like there is a lot of stuff in a small space. Most of the items in the bathroom are more than likely used on a regular basis, so getting rid of them is simply not an option. However, it looks like the cosmetic section at the store blew up in there. There are ways to unclutter these spaces while not getting rid of the items that you don't want to sacrifice.

Decluttering and simplifying doesn't necessarily mean getting rid of everything you own. It also has a lot to do with organization and where items are kept. By rearranging your spaces, you can quite possibly declutter and simplify without having to donate half of your life to the thrift store. Let's take a look at some ways that you can declutter and organize your living space in order to achieve a happier atmosphere.

*Bathroom Organization Tools*

Every bathroom that I have ever been in has had extremely limited counter space. With so much that I need in my personal beauty routine, how do I deal with not having a counter to spread out on? After careful thought, I decided that I would use other resources in my bathroom that can help me to stay organized and make my bathroom look tidy.

I began by using the wall space. For my styling tools, such as my straightener and blow dryer, I installed hooks on the wall in which I could hang them from their cords when they are not in use. Even if you have tools with retractable cords, you can use something to attach the tool to the hook, such as a piece of strong string.

After I made good use of my wall space, I cleared up my cluttered counters by using small shelves on the walls in which I could store lotions and hair supplies. These helped get them up and off the counter when not in use. All of the other tools I was able to purchase a small set of plastic drawers that I could toss them in and get them out of the way.

*Creating Space in Your Closet*

Closet space is often the most limited space in your home, and you will more than likely store more stuff in there than in the rest of your home. Before you try to create space, try to get rid of some of the items that make it cluttered. If you were to dig to the back of your closet, you would probably find items that you forgot you even had. Get rid of them and that opens up space right there. After you have gotten rid of what you can, then try using shelving and hooks to store what is being kept. Getting some of the items off the floor and off of the hangers can help you to create more space.

*Making the Most of Your Storage Space*

Even when simplifying, we will still have some items that will require storage. These often include seasonal items, and you will use them again when that holiday or season comes around. Try storing like items together, using as few storage containers as you possibly can. You might have to get creative with the packing, but the more you can fit in a box, the more space you will save. Also, try to make sure that all of your storage containers are the same size. This will make them easy to stack and create a cleaner and simpler appearance to your storage area.

Even though your personal areas are not seen on a regular basis, they still need to be simplified and cut back in order to make your home much more breathable. Closets and storage areas can quickly be torn into and cause the rest of the home to feel cluttered again. Don't let your personal space clutter your common space. This will only set you up for a vicious cycle that will see no end!

# Chapter 4- Tips for Simplifying Your Decor

You may have a lot of personal family memories that you want to display in your home. However, there is a point where your décor can become a little too much. Clutter can happen on your walls and shelves, making it hard to see past the stuff and enjoy the simplicity of life. If you cannot see the wall behind the pictures and decorations, you probably have too much going on. Everyone walking into your home is probably on sensory overload. Would you want to walk into a place that has too much going on?

It might be time for you to put some of those memories away and simplify your décor. Think about walking into your home and what you would really like for it to look like. Do you enjoy having a simple and eye-pleasing décor? Then try to make your home reflect this idea. In this chapter, we are going to take a look at some ways that you can still hold onto some of those family memories while simplifying your home décor.

*Make a Photo Collage*

Many people have family photos that they wish to display on their walls. However, if you have a large family or multiple photos, this could be a quick way to clutter your walls and make for sensory overload for whoever views them. If you really want to keep these pictures on display, then try creating a photo collage of them. You can group photos by event, person, or any other them and put them in a collage frame.

This will solve the problem of wall clutter and still give you the benefit of displaying your beloved photos.

*Repurpose Your Favorite Decoration Pieces*

As you find yourself simplifying your living area and décor, try altering your favorite decorations so that they have a new and fresh feel to them. You might have a wreath that you can add a few baubles to and make it feel updated and different. Being creative with your décor can offer you a simpler look while cutting back on the clutter that is in your home. Reusing and refreshing what you have in creative ways can make your home feel more unique.

*Change Your Theme*

If you find that your current theme jumped out of the seventies, you may want to consider a change. While some people appreciate bright colors and vivid décor, the simpler you make it, the more inviting it will be. It's okay to have a few accent pieces, but make sure that your main theme is simple. Again, this is easy to accomplish by using earth tones as your color base and building around that. You don't have to add too much to your room to make it classy. In fact, a lot of people think that the less a room has, the better that it looks! Not only are you saving yourself clutter, you are also saving yourself some time when it comes to cleaning a wide array of unnecessary items. This is time that you can do what you enjoy with!

*Reupholster Your Furniture*

You don't have to get rid of your favorite sofa just because the coloring isn't simple and doesn't fit your décor. Try reupholstering it to make it fit into your room and making it simple. This will give you the simple and fresh feel you desire without giving up what you love. A simple pattern can help your home feel fresh and uncluttered. Try looking at this possibility before you invest in all new furniture!

*Bring in Natural Elements*

In a simple life, you don't want your home to feel too complex in any way. This includes your possessions and your décor. Try bringing in the feeling of nature into your home. Use natural light when possible, and get rid of anything that feels unnecessary and cluttering. By getting rid of items and cutting back on what you own, you can easily allow the simplicity of natural elements to invade your space.

*Minimize Your Furniture*

While furniture may be a great convenience, it can also be a great burden. It takes up space, might not even be used, and it might just cause clutter in your home. For example, my spouse loves books. We have numerous bookshelves in our living room. I know that he will never read all of those books. By getting rid of these books and bookshelves, I can really cut back the clutter in my living room and simplify my living space. Now, I just need to convince him that he doesn't need all those books…

*Minimize Your Decorations*

I love bric a brac and anything cute that can adorn my shelves. However, when I decided to cut back on this type of items, my home felt less cluttered. While some of these items are sentimental to me, most of them have no value whatsoever. By getting rid of most of my unnecessary and cluttering decorations, I found that I actually enjoy my home more than I did before. I can still enjoy the cute in passing, but I won't bring in home anymore to adorn my shelves.

Cutting back on your décor and simplifying what you do have are great ways to simplify your life and feel like you live for more than stuff. Keeping your possessions and your home simple will help you to focus on more important aspects of your life. Plus, the simpler your home is, the easier it is to clean! That is incentive enough for me to simplify!

# Chapter 5- Tips for Organizing Your Storage Areas

Most of us don't believe that we have enough storage for the items that we wish to store. We may look at areas such as our garage, our linen closets or even our bedroom closets and think that it looks like a tornado has ripped through them. Finding places to put things will ultimately lead to clutter, and clutter is a huge eyesore. Plus, when we wish to find something, we will tear apart our storage area until we locate it.

In order to downsize, we must get rid of this clutter. This can mean giving items up to thrift stores, having a garage sale or using them as hand me downs. However you decide that you want to downsize and cut back, you will be glad you did once you see the space you have found. However, for the items that you wish to continue to store, organization can play a key factor in making sure that your home doesn't become a tornado when you want to find just one item. In this chapter, I'm going to cover some creative storage organization ideas that might help you to feel like it isn't a catch all.

*Hooks and Shelves*

Once you have decluttered your storage areas, it is important that you find ways to organize it so that it won't create problems for you in the future. In your storage closets, attics and garages, try using shelves and hooks on the walls to help you organize what you wish to store. By having everything in a certain place, you will take the guess work out of finding an item when you actually need it. Shelves can help accommodate your storage in multiple ways because they can be placed in such a way that you can put anything you wish upon them.

*Hanging Items at Different Heights*

Using your wall space can have great benefits to decluttering and organizing your storage areas. For items that can be hung on the wall, use hooks at different levels to help you to create a more organized and simple method to storing these items. When you wish to get an item that is hanging, you can find it much easier if it is at a different level than other items in your storage area.

*Storage Bins and Drawers*

Bins and drawers help out a lot in decluttering and storing items, especially those that will not work out well in boxes and hanging on walls. By investing in a few small storage bins and drawers, you can easily organize the small items that you have in your storage areas. Be careful that you continue to group like items together, making it easier for you to find them when you need them!

*Labeling*

In order to simplify your storage experience, try labeling your boxes, bins and drawers using a label machine or laminated cards. This will help guide you in organizing and finding what you wish to find in your storage areas. This will also help you to put your items back in the places where they belong without creating more clutter in your life. Why not prevent your simple and decluttered home from returning to its original state?

*Categorize Your Stored Items*

Once you have your items in boxes and labeled, it's important that you put like items together. For example, you will want to store seasonal decorations apart from winter clothing. This will allow you to know where to find what you want when you go looking for it. Don't make simplifying your life difficult and frustrating!

*Make Use of Your Space*

When you store items, it's important that you make use of the space given without cluttering it. Evaluate your storage area and determine how you can stack, build shelves, or install hooks in order to make your storage experience as pain free as possible.

Organizing and decluttering your storage space can really help you simplify your life in many ways. Not having to spend hours searching for one item or having to rip apart the closet will make it worth it for you in the long run. By cutting back and organizing, you are simplifying your life in ways that will help you for years to come.

# Chapter 6- Tips for Simplifying Your Closets

As I write this book, I'm thinking about my bedroom closet. It looks like a clothing store threw up and the shoes were the unfortunate victims of an explosion. As much as I would like to say that my closet is organized by garment type and color, that would be a lie. How can I possibly make my closet look like it would be featured on television? No matter how many times I have tried to organize this area of my home, the end result remains the same. I still end up with a mess.

For this chapter, I turn to other resources for ideas on how to make my closets more organized keep them that way. Some of the ideas I will be soon trying out in my own situation. I will also provide some tips on how to organize other closets in your home. Let's try some of these tips and see if we can achieve more organized and simply closets!

*Layering Hangers*

I have seen this suggestion in multiple places. What you do is take soda can tabs and place them over the hook of a hanger. You can then hang another hanger from the tab, allowing you to store more than one garment and not take up closet space. This can come in handy when it comes to storing outfits, putting the top on the top hanger and the pants on the lower hanger.

*Have Shelving for Your Shoes*

If you have a lot of shoes, then having shoe shelves in your closet can have a huge effect on how organized your closet looks and will make it feel less cluttered. When looking for a pair of shoes, if you have shelves, you can easily view what you have instead of digging through a huge pile and creating a larger mess.

*Store Only What Your Closet is Intended for*

While it might feel convenient to store whatever you want to get out of sight in your bedroom closet, all you are accomplishing is creating clutter and making your closet a catch all. Make your closet for your clothing and shoes only. By limiting what you are storing in your closet to what needs to be there, you are stopping yourself from dealing with another annoying clutter situation in the future.

*Get Rid of Unnecessary Items*

If you haven't worn it or used it in six months, get rid of it. The number one cause of clutter is keeping something that we believe that we will use again, when in reality, we probably won't. Donate your unworn clothing, shoes, and linens to thrift shops so that they can benefit others. Not only are you solving your clutter problem, you are preventing yourself from facing future clutter problems. Plus, you are simplifying your life by being able to know what you have and where it is.

*Employ Plastic Drawers*

Plastic drawers in closet spaces are a nice way to do away with the dresser. You can hang most of your clothing and store what you can't in plastic drawers. These are easy to see into, and they will help you remain organized in your closet area. You can also use these to store bathroom and jewelry items to help you in finding them when needed.

*Have an Organizational Method that will Allow You to Return All Items to the Same Place*

While you may think that your organization will last for a while, it will quickly go back to what it was if you don't put your items back where they belong. Having a place for everything and putting everything in its place may seem cliché, but it really can help you to maintain a simple life. Once you have an organizational system that you like, find ways to put your items back and keep them where they need to be. This will not only save you time, it will save you the trouble of having to reorganize on a regular basis. While it might seem like an inconvenience to return items to their places all the time, just think of the time that it took you to organize it in the first place!

Since closets can easily become a catch all for things we wish to not see, having a way to organize them and keep them from becoming cluttered can be a huge help in making sure that your efforts are not in vain. Make sure that you use your closets for their intended purposes, whether it be for clothing or for linens. When other items make their way into these areas, it is bound to lead to clutter. Make your life simpler by changing your habits and keeping your decluttered area continuously decluttered!

# Chapter 7- Downsizing for Your Sanity

When we have too much stuff, stuff can overtake our lives. It may not seem that way, but when you have to give up your enjoyment and favorite activities to organize and declutter your home, you are losing out on a life that you really deserve to be living. I don't think I have ever met a person who enjoys cleaning and organizing their home. This task is an as necessary task, and it usually gets performed about once a year. It is time consuming and frustrating.

You might want to ask yourself why you are stressing out over material possessions. After all, they mean very little to you in the grand scheme of things, so why put your time and effort into gaining and keeping them? The less you have, the happier you will be. Also, the less you have, the easier it is to keep your home clean and organized. Just thinking about these aspects of decluttering makes me want to jump up and start shoving unnecessary items into boxes for donation!

Getting rid of your unnecessary junk will help you to cut back on the stuff that causes you such a headache when it comes to cleaning and organizing. Since we have become so used to living for material possessions, we often miss out on the most important things in our lives. Don't allow stuff to take your life away. Get rid of it and simplify your life. Yes, you will still need items to live, but what you have probably is much more than what you really need.

You only have one life to live, so you need to make the most of it. If you find that your time is centered on possessions, then it's time for you to cut back and simplify. I have just started this process myself, and I have found the work that I have already done very rewarding. By cutting back on my possessions and simplifying my home, I have found that it is more aesthetically pleasing and I have less cleaning and upkeep to worry about. Having less stuff means that I don't have to clean it! I love that about living a simpler life!

Also, having a home and a life that you dream of is a goal that is well worth reaching. No one wants to look at their home and see visions of hoarders. It's just stuff, and you cannot take it with you when you die. So, what's the point in living for it? Take time to live your life and do the things that you enjoy. Allow your relationships to grow and spend time with those you care about. Don't allow your home and your possessions to stand in the way of living the life that you dream of.

If you haven't started to declutter and cut back on your possessions, I highly encourage you to. Take the time and get rid of what you don't need and limit what you do need. Get yourself organized and keep yourself that way. I assure you that once you find the simple life, you will love it and won't think about building up your stock of possessions again.

It could help your mindset to have a life that is free from clutter and free from worries about the clutter. Why not try to cut back and simplify? You might find that you enjoy your life much more once you make this change!

# Conclusion

I hope this book was able to help you to find ways to declutter and simplify your life. People live for possessions without even realizing it. Why not live for something meaningful and place the junk aside?

The next step is to find ways to cut back and simplify in your home or office. By getting rid of the extras, you will find that you will enjoy your life much more!

# DOWNSIZING YOUR LIFE AND LOVING IT

## 50 CREATIVE WAYS TO DECLUTTER YOUR SPACE, LIVE WITH LESS AND SIMPLIFY YOUR LIFE

### KATHY STANTON

# Introduction

This book contains proven steps and strategies on how to minimalize your belongings, chore list, and thoughts in order to give you a more fulfilling and simplistic life. If you're like most people, you probably have way more than you really need. This isn't limited to possessions, but chores and thoughts. In a society where more is emphasized, living simple is difficult.

Have you found that you have way too much going on in your life? You find that your possessions outnumber your needs and you have a to do list that stretches on and on. Your life is consumed. Have you ever thought of what it would feel like to have less? If you could minimalize your stresses, would you? This book focuses on ways to simplify your life so that you can reduce stress and love life.

# Chapter 1- What is Too Much in Life?

Have you noticed that this society emphasizes success by how much you have rather than happiness? I have found that I hate the fact that my success is based upon how much I have. Sure, it might be nice to have the new gadgets and everything you could possibly want, but in the end, is it really worth it? No possession or amount of activity can really satisfy your need for success.

Success is defined differently for different people. Sure, some might thrive off of having more and more. However, our human nature isn't dependent upon having excess. We have simple needs that we need met, but beyond that, everything is just considered a luxury. When we make our luxuries into needs, then we tend to be unhappy.

I have evaluated my life and found that getting rid of the extras makes me feel happier. I'm not stressed out with trying to obtain more and what I have is sufficient. When I finally came to that mindset, it was a huge relief. I didn't feel like I needed to do everything in order to accomplish a goal that wasn't even necessary.

How about you? Do you find that you're stressed out by thinking about all you have to do in order to maintain what you have? Take a close look at your life. Do you have excess that you're trying to maintain? Are there things that you can do without? If your answer to any of these questions is "yes," I encourage you to read this book and reevaluate what is really a need as opposed to what is a luxury. What you might find out about yourself might surprise you.

If you're looking to simplify your life, I encourage you to continue reading. In this book, I'm going to give you some hints and tips on how to get rid of the excess so that you can enjoy what you have. You might find that the simple life is the way to go and love it as much as I do!

# Chapter 2- Evaluating Need versus Want

The first step to finding a simple life is looking at what is before you. Some things you have you would consider a need, while other things are considered clutter and could easily be done away with. For some, they consider things as needs what others would easily be able to get rid of. Since every person is different, I want to look at the criteria for what a need is as opposed to a want. I'm not saying it's wrong to have items you want. However, when your life becomes dependent on keeping a certain standard of life that is unnecessary, then it becomes a stress for you and an inhibitor to the simple lifestyle.

So, I encourage you to be brutally honest with yourself when looking at the items in your life. If you find that you have more of what you want than what you actually need, you might want to reevaluate your priorities in order to simplify your life.

*When Was the Last Time I Used It?*

This is a big question for me. The items that I think that I need usually end up sitting in a drawer or closet. When I bought them, I thought that they would be useful, but in the end, I never even used them! Do you find things in your home that you have lightly or never used? I would consider these things a want rather than a need. These are the items that I would try to weed out of my life first.

*Do I Really Want to Put the Extra Effort into Maintaining it if I Don't Need it?*

Some people thrive upon having luxurious items. They are willing to work hard for them, and they will do whatever they can to keep them. However, some of these things are just not worth the effort. For example, you have a car that you really like, but it tends to break down a lot. You spend a lot of time and money trying to keep it in working order. When asked whether or not you consider this a need, you would say yes. So, you are willing to put forth the extra effort and time to maintain your luxury. If it is something that you really want and would consider a need, then by all means, keep it.

*If I were to Toss it Out, Would I Miss It?*

Before I decided to simplify my life and home, I would constantly come across items that I had no idea I even owned. They were probably some impulse buy that I thought that I would use later. However, they soon ended up getting stored and forgotten about. I need to ask myself when I encounter such objects one pressing question; "Will I miss it if it were not here?" For most of these things, it would be a resounding "YES!" For others, I really did need it, but ultimately forgot to use it. In a busy, cluttered life, that sometimes happens.

*Does it Make Me Happy?*

In the previous chapter, we talked about success and happiness and how people tend to connect the two with belongings. So, at this time, I want you to look at some of you major belongings and ask yourself whether or not they make you happy. For the most part, I bet that most of the answers will be "no." General happiness is not dependent upon what you have, but on the other factors in your life and how they all work together.

*If I Were to Have Nothing, What Would I Need to Survive?*

Let's do a little test. Imagine that your home was destroyed in some freak natural disaster. You literally have nothing to your name except the clothing on your back. What would you need at that point in time? Thing about the basic pyramid of needs. You probably would be thinking about food, shelter, and other practical items that would help you to survive. Odds are, you won't be thinking about replacing your laptop or the earrings that your husband gave you for your anniversary. What you have just evaluated was what is a true need as opposed to a luxury. You can live without a laptop computer and jewelry. You can't live without food or shelter.

The next time you look around your home, ask yourself some of these questions. You might be surprised at the sheer volume of goods that you own that you really could live without. Try making a change to a simple life by weeding out the luxuries and focusing on the needs. In the following chapters, I'm going to give you hints on how to simplify your life in a few different ways. Items are not the only things that keep us from enjoy simple living!

# Chapter 3- How to Reduce Your Belongings

As highlighted in the previous chapter, our belongings tend to be the number one thing that keeps us from having a simple life. Even though they are just stuff, we tend to form emotional bonds with this stuff that can be difficult to break.

However, it might be necessary to break these bond if you're looking to simplify your life. This can take some time and patience on your part. No one wants to admit that something that they really like is nothing more than a thing. So, I'm going to give you some tips and hints on how to reduce your belongings in order to live a happier life.

*Go Through Everything You Own*

Depending upon how much you own, this can be quite the undertaking. However, it will be necessary in order to downsize your belongings to a manageable level. The first thing that I recommend is that you go through each and every item you own. Take a close look at them, and separate them into piles. Have a pile for what you will for sure keep, one for the maybes, and one to get rid of. Do this room by room so that your house won't look like a total and complete wreck. The items that you can safely say that you need to keep can be put back right away and you can evaluate the rest of it later on.

*Evaluate whether what you have before you is needed*

This is a test of your will. Take some time and look at your stuff. Ask yourself whether or not you really need the item and whether or not you will ever use the item on a regular basis. Imagine how your life would be without it. If you can safely say that you really don't need it, get rid of it. It's better to be honest with yourself and do it all at once than finding out later that you kept something around that resulted in clutter.

*Donate or Sell Your Excess Stuff*

This is another necessary part to your puzzle. Now is the time to get rid of the items that you have decided that you don't need. I prefer to donate them to a thrift store or have a garage sale. For some, donating it is the easiest option. For me, I enjoy having a yearly garage sale and getting rid of things. Not only does it make me money, but I also have the chance to invite friends or family to bring their stuff and it's like a reunion. However, arranging a garage sale can be time consuming and stressful if you don't go about it in the right way.

*Have Someone Help You*

Some people refuse to seek help. However, if you're living with others, they need to be on the same page as you, so enlisting their help will be necessary. Even if you live alone, having a friend come over and help you to get rid of some unnecessary stuff can both be fun and helpful. You never know, your friend might just take some of that stuff off of your hands for you and that's one less worry later on!

Asking for help is not a sign of weakness. It's simply saying that you want to make a change and that you want another person to be a part of that change. So, don't worry about someone thinking you're weak for asking for help. You're just trying to do what is best for you.

*Give it to Family or Friends*

Having younger (or older) siblings can be another fun way to get rid of your unwanted belongings. For me, I have a sister who loves my tastes in clothing and home décor, so when I asked if she wanted to come over and take some of the items I was getting rid of, she was excited. You might have a friend who is like that for you. Knowing someone who shares your tastes is a good way to recycle some of the old stuff you intend to get rid of. If you have some family or friends who would love to relieve you of your excess belongings, don't be afraid to ask them! It could benefit both of you.

*Be Heartless*

This is one tip that has helped me along the way. Since I base a lot of emotional value on some of my belongings, when I go to get rid of them, I find that I doubt my decision based upon that bond. It could be something that I got with my mother that brings back memories. However, this is something I have to look past. Look at the item for what it is. Will you need it or use it? Can you live without it? Be heartless and rip the memories that are associated with object away from it. In the end, it's just a piece of stuff that will clutter your home. Remember that!

*If You Haven't used it in Six Months, Trash it*

Another great method that I use to declutter my home is to look at what is before me and evaluate whether or not I have used this item in the past six months. If I haven't used or looked at it that long, I haven't missed it. I will put it into my donation pile. The biggest mistake that you can make is to look at the object and tell yourself that you will use it again. You won't, so don't keep it around. Six months is a reasonable time span to realize whether or not you will actually use it.

*Downsize Your Home*

For some of us, we live in a home that is much too big for our needs. If possible, downsize your living quarters to something that is more manageable to clean and furnish. I understand that moving is not feasible for all, but if you have the opportunity to downsize your home, you will also be forced to get rid of some of your belongings when you move. Think about it. This might be the way to go!

Downsizing your possessions can be a tough and time consuming process. No one likes to get rid of their things. After all, you chose them and worked hard to buy them. However, when your life becomes complicated because of your need to maintain your possessions, you're not going to be happy. Try decluttering and downsizing in the area of your possessions and see how much better you feel by making this change.

This is a process. Don't overwhelm yourself with getting rid of all the items you don't need at once. This will make the whole idea seem even more overwhelming than just keeping the stuff in your life. So, I recommend that you take this process in pieces. It could take you a few months to make it through. However long it takes, know that you're making a positive step towards simplifying your life with the shedding of your excess possessions.

# Chapter 4- Cutting Back on Your Chore List

Another good way to encourage simple living is by cutting back on the list of things that you feel you have to have done. People tend to put too much on themselves, making it more difficult to have time for what really matters. Depending on your lifestyle and personality, you will value your time differently. If you feel like you're spending too much time doing mundane chores, then maybe it's time to reevaluate your priorities and make time for what really matters instead of filling your time with nonsense.

In this chapter, I am going to give you some hints as to how to cut out chores from your busy schedule in order to make more time for what really matters to you. So, if you would like to simplify your time, then let's take a look at some ways to make that happen!

*Does it Really Need to be done?*

Some tasks are necessary in order to run your household. Others are simply fillers. When you look at your day and the list that you have compiled that you want to get done, think about whether or not the task must get done in order to maintain your life, or if it's something that you choose to do.

By being honest with yourself and realizing that you're picking up too much on your to do list, you will be on your way to saying that some tasks are unnecessary and clutter your time.

*Can You Have Someone Else do it?*

When did it become a fact that you do all the chores? If you live with multiple people, this is unfair and stressful to you. Take a look at your day as opposed to the others you live with.

Can someone else do the task on the list? If you're like me and try to do it all, then there is definitely someone who will be able to help you by taking on the task and completing it. So, the next time you feel overwhelmed by the to do list, think about this factor. Have someone help you!

*What Would you do with Some Free Time?*

Feel free to daydream a little bit. What would you do if you found some extra free time within your day? Well, by simplifying your chore list, you might be able to make this daydream a possibility. Don't be afraid to think about how you would spend your time if you didn't have a million things to do. It can really work out that you can have that time if you learn to manage your time properly and leave out unnecessary tasks.

*What Activities Would You Like to Spend Your Time Doing?*

Going along with the question above, think about ways you would like to spend your time. You probably don't want to be spending great amounts of time working in order to maintain a luxurious lifestyle that you could easily do without. Surprisingly enough, people do this every day. They work hard in order to buy things and do things that they cannot afford. It's okay to do some things you want to do, but don't make it so extreme that you end up working more than you need to in order to get there!

*Respect Your Time and That of Others*

In today's world, we look out for number one and try to focus on helping everyone else at the same time. If you're one of these people, you will give your time to help anyone in need. This can be a positive thing, but it can easily turn into something negative. People who realize that you will do whatever you want them to do will use you for that reason. They will have little regard for your time, but focus on what you can do for them. On the flip side, you might be that person who expects that from others. The biggest tip I can give here is respect your own time and that of others. Once you learn that your time is valuable and their time is too, you will be finding that you can maintain a healthier balance in your schedule.

*Plan What is Necessary and Leave Out the Unnecessary*

Life is unpredictable. I get that. However, having a plan to your day can be very helpful in making sure that you accomplish the necessary tasks. Other stuff will come up throughout the day. Take it as it comes. However, if you're planning on doing things that are not necessary for you, then you are filling your day with clutter. The point it to get away from this clutter so that you can have a healthy and happy life.

*Don't Allow Others' Opinions of You to Dominate Your Time and Your Lifestyle*

People are opinionated beings. If you ask every person in your life for suggestions on how to live yours, you will get as many answers as people. They aren't living your life though. You are. So, when you begin to think about what someone else is going to think about what you're doing, let those thoughts slip away. If you live your life based upon someone else's opinions, you're not living your own life, but theirs. Let them live the way they want and you live the way you want. Don't allow other people's opinions to dictate how you live your life.

By making some changes to your schedule and what you choose to do on a daily basis, you can simplify your life and make yourself happier because you will have more time to do what you want to do. Your schedule is a huge part of your day, so being able to cut out the unnecessary factors will make it easier for you to have time for what you would like to do and spend time with those who you value.

Time is a tricky thing. We find ourselves wasting it frequently and then wishing we could have it back. If you find that you tend to waste more time than using it productively, try to make some changes to your schedule that will open up time for what is necessary and what you would enjoy doing.

# Chapter 5- Simplifying Your Thought Life

If you're anything like me, then your mind is always running on overdrive. When I'm not thinking about one thing, another thought consumes my mind. There is no peace when you are constantly thinking. Have you ever tried to simplify your thoughts so that you can have a peaceful existence? It is impossible, but you will need to learn to train your brain to make it happen. This can be done in a number of ways, but depending on how you operate, you might find one way works much better than another.

In this chapter, I'm going to give you some advice on how to simplify your thoughts in order to downsize the amount of stress in your life. When you have tranquil thoughts, then you will be able to have a less stressful and turbulent existence.

*Meditate*

When you find that you cannot concentrate on anything because your mind is so consumed with other thoughts, take a moment out of your time and meditate. There are a number of things that you can meditate on. Think about your religion, your friends, your family, or even your pets. Find something that will center you when you begin to feel your mind go out of control. By focusing on this, the random and irritating thoughts will ease themselves out of your mind and you can focus on the tasks at hand.

*Prayer*

If you follow a religion, praying is a great way to focus your energy and thought process. By taking a few moments and talking to God, you will find that you will feel yourself calm down and that the thoughts will go away. When you have too much going on in your head, taking time to let some of that stress out is helpful to your happiness and to your thoughts.

*Push the Negative Thoughts Away*

Some people find that the thoughts that flood their minds are negative and self-defeating. If you're the type of person who tends to have a negative thought life, then it's time to put those thoughts aside and let positive ones in. It's difficult to break a bad habit of negative thinking once it begins. However, try to break the pattern by pushing those negative thoughts out of your head and trying to replace them with happier thoughts. You will never have a happy life if your mind is cluttered by negative thoughts!

*Focus on the Moment*

Focus is one of the ways that you can make your thought processes simpler and more fulfilling. I find that I tend to let my mind wander when the topic of my focus isn't exciting or thought-provoking. However, if I were to focus on the moment, I would get that task done quicker and then I would have time to think about other things. If you lack focus on what you need to do, then you will only draw out the process and make it longer than it really needs to be.

*Push Away the "What if" Mentality*

I'm a daydreamer and I will admit that. However, I will keep myself awake at night thinking about what would happen if I would have done something differently. Don't beat yourself up about what has already happened. If your thoughts are consumed by this type of thinking, it's time for you to break that habit. The what ifs will only make you miserable and rob you of time that you could be spending doing other tasks.

*Stop Random Thinking When it Begins*

If your mind tends to wander, then try to stop it from going to places it doesn't need to be before it has a chance to go there. There are certain triggers that will get me to start thinking about random circumstances. Once I identified these triggers,

I was able to stop the random thoughts before they even had a chance to begin. Think about things that will divert your attention and recognize them if you have trouble focusing on what needs to be done. Knowing these diversions will make it easier for you to push them away when necessary.

*Learn to Say No to Your Thoughts*

Sometimes, random thoughts do creep in. You start by asking yourself whether or not you should go and do an activity later on. Before you know it, you will be thinking about doing this activity, the ramifications of the activity, what it will entail, and any number of thoughts that surround it. However, you're supposed to be focused on another task. That task is being pushed aside for your random thoughts. So, learn how to say no to your thoughts when you notice that they can lead you down a path that will lead to distraction. If the thought is important, jot it down and come back to it when you have time to think about it.

Life tends to be more complicated when we think more than we should about things we shouldn't be thinking about. We all do it. Depending on how you handle the thoughts and choose to get rid of them will determine your mind's declutter process. Yes, your mind can be just as cluttered as your schedule or your home. By learning to simplify your thought process, you will discover that you will have more freedom to get what needs to be done accomplished and have time to do what you would like to do afterwards.

Thoughts are a difficult territory to control. We are used to our thoughts taking us wherever they want to, and trying to tell them they can't do that can be a long and frustrating process. However, you will find that simplifying your thoughts will increase your ability to lead a simple and happier lifestyle.

# Chapter 6- Enjoying what Matters

If you have found that you don't have much time to enjoy your life, then it's quite possible that you have too much stuff going on. Whether it be too much stuff or too many thoughts, something is making it so that you cannot enjoy what really matters to you. It might take some time to figure out what is making your life so complicated and stressful, but once you do, you will be able to make the necessary changes in order to live a simpler, more fulfilling life.

After discussing how to rid yourself of all the extra stuff in your life, I'd like to take this chapter to focus on how to enjoy what matters to you once you have cleared out the clutter of life. Again, this might be a stage that will take some time to reach, but once you're there, you will be happier and more fulfilled with your life.

*Plan Fun Activities with Those You Care About*

Instead of cluttering your day with things that really don't matter, plan activities with friends and family that you will enjoy. Simply getting together with a friend for a cup of coffee can make your day much more enjoyable and take some of the hustle and bustle from your life. Before our society got so busy and complicated, people spent more time together. Try this and see if it will make you feel happier and more content.

## Take Time to Enjoy the Moment

When our lives are busy and hectic, we don't have the opportunity to enjoy the moment for what it really is. Take that time to enjoy the beauty of a summer day while walking to work. Find things to appreciate in the small areas of life. If you can find positive things to enjoy about whatever you're doing, you will find that your life will feel more complete and more fulfilling. Like the old saying goes, "Take time to smell the roses." Take some time to enjoy the small and simple things in life.

## Take Time for What You Want to Do

You might feel that you're being selfish by doing this, but by taking time to do what you enjoy can have a huge impact on your life. This can be a simple thing that you enjoy doing on a daily basis that will help you to enjoy your day. Maybe you like the extra flavored creamer in your coffee, so you use it when you feel like you might have a rough day. Whatever you want to do, give yourself the satisfaction of doing it. It will help you to enjoy your life more.

## Don't Allow Others to Dominate Your Time

We talked a little about this in a previous chapter. If you're the type of person who will bend over backwards to help someone, you will get taken advantage of by the wrong people. When that happens, they will dominate your time with their needs and you won't have time to take care of your own needs. This is not only robbing you of your time, but it also enables them to use others instead of being self-sufficient. Don't be afraid to say no to someone who obviously can fend for himself. You aren't being cruel, you're just making it so that you can have your time and the other person will learn to do for himself.

*Allow Yourself the Freedom to Enjoy Your Time*

I know that I find myself feeling guilty when I get time to myself. I always feel like I could be doing something else to help someone else. However, if I don't look out for myself, then I am ultimately running myself toward a condition of being burnt out. Take some time to do what you enjoy and give yourself the freedom to enjoy that time without feeling guilty. Sadly enough, most of us don't get that freedom in our lives, and it is necessary to keep ourselves happy and centered.

Learning to enjoy the changes that you make in your life is crucial to making your simple life work for you. If you make changes to your life and they go without notice, then you have wasted your time. So, when you pursue that simple life, learn to find ways to enjoy your life. Like I stated above, you can simply enjoy a walk from your car to your place of employment. It's the simple things in life that really make it more enjoyable.

One of the biggest obstacles that you will endure when trying to enjoy your time is the feeling of guilt that you're not helping someone else. The sooner you realize that you need to take care of yourself before you can help others, the sooner you will be free to enjoy a simple life and love it.

# Chapter 7- Loving Your Simple Life

Life isn't meant to be complicated and stressful. We make it that way with what we choose to do with our lives. So, by realizing that your life doesn't have to be complicated, you're ready to pursue a simple and enjoyable life!

Now that you're on your way to finding out how a simple life can benefit your way of thinking and how you live your life, you can begin to enjoying your simple life. Since you're so used to making decisions based upon a busy and full life, having time to enjoy the simple things in life might be new concept to you. What would you do if you could take a breath and enjoy life for what it is?

Let me tell you a little bit about my own experience. Now that I don't have the stress of providing a lifestyle beyond my means, I am much happier. I love the fact that I don't have to worry about how I'm going to pay my bills, what I need to buy, and who will judge me for my simple life. Since I have found that we tend to put on a show for the rest of the world, not doing so has made a huge impact on how I enjoy my life. It's my life and no one else's opinions matter.

Once you take the next step and realize that you don't need the world to be happy, you will be on your way to finding your happiness. By getting rid of all the excess, you are actually gaining more. You will have more time, more quality to your relationships, and less stress. Those all sound great, right?

If you haven't thought about pursuing a simpler lifestyle, then I encourage you to give it a try. There are many people I know of who are taking the next steps to getting rid of the excess in their lives and I can already see a difference in their lives. They just seem happier and more fulfilled.

Take the chance at being happy. Downsize and see how it can benefit you. I'm living a simple lifestyle and loving it, and I'm sure you will too if you will give it a chance. Good luck!

# Conclusion

I hope this book was able to help you to find ways to simplify your life through getting rid of unnecessary thoughts, possessions, and chores. We tend to make our lives much more complicated without meaning to. By having a simple life, we can learn to enjoy our lives much more.

The next step is to figure out areas in your life that are complicated. By knowing what you would like to change about your life, you will be prepared to take steps to simplify your day and love it!

Finally, if you enjoyed this book, then I'd like to ask you for a favor, would you be kind enough to leave a review for this book on Amazon? It'd be greatly appreciated!

# SPENDING LESS AND LOVING IT

## 50 Creative Ways To Manage Your Money, Set Up A Budget And Achieve Financial Success

**KATHY STANTON**

# Introduction

This book contains proven steps and strategies on how to make an effective budget so that you can experience financial freedom. Many people find that they are living beyond their means. By managing your budget and only spending what you have, you can make a huge difference in the way you live and how you view your financial resources.

Many people struggle with financial stress because they lack the ability to manage their financial resources. However, if people had ways to learn to budget their money and monitor their spending, then they would be better able to achieve financial success. In this book, I'm going to offer you some tips and strategies on how to save money by creating a budget that will work with your lifestyle.

# Chapter 1- The Makings of a Budget

In a society where money has little to no meaning on a daily basis, people tend to spend what they want, when they want to. Why this might be nice at the time, when it comes to the end of the month, people are often short on finances and stress in order to make the bills happen. If only they would have thought through their purchases prior to initiating them, they might have avoided the problem in the first place. So, how do people make sure that they have all the money they need in order to not stress at the end of a month?

The answer is called a budget. Having one of these handy tools at your fingertips can really influence how and where you spend your money on a daily basis. The sad part of the matter is, not many people understand or know how to budget their money in order to achieve financial success. It's my goal to help you understand what makes up a budget and how using one can drastically improve your financial situation and cash flow.

So, let's start at the beginning and analyze what a budget is and how to build one to suit your personal needs. Once you have a firm understanding of budgeting, you will be able to build your own and see the benefits it can initiate in your life.

A budget is essentially a tool that shows you where your money goes and where your money comes from. It then takes your income and subtracts your expenses from it, showing you if you have money left at the end of the month, or if you are going to be short on funds. Once you have all of your bills plugged into this budget, you can really see where your money goes and where changes need to be made in order to ensure that you do have money left at the end of the month.

Building a budget is quite simple, and your computer's office documents will have templates to help you make your own budget. These spreadsheets will calculate your findings for you, taking the guesswork out of the process. If you have the resource, try plugging in your expenses and income and see what it tells you.

One thing that you really need to keep in mind when building a budget is the miscellaneous money you spend that you might not even realize is leaving your hand. Think about when you stop to grab a cup of coffee or a soda. These transactions do affect your budget, even though they seem petty and small. Adding the two to three dollars you spent at the coffee shop could influence your budget if you do it repeatedly.

So, when building a budget, include every time you spend money or take make money. Every penny can affect your overall financial situation, even if it seems like a small and unworthy transaction. If it helps, try looking at your bank statements and see where you used your card or withdrew money from the ATM. These all add up in the end, and just a few dollars could make a huge difference when you need to pay that power bill at the end of the month!

Are you ready to build your own budget? Then round up your receipts and bills, and let's see where your money is going. If it's a shock to you, then it may be a wonderful time to change your spending habits in order to be able to save money and see a positive figure at the end of the month.

In the following chapters, I'm going to give you some tips and advice on ways you can spend less money so that you can have a positive-looking budget. I'm also going to get a little creative in how to spend your money and ways you can spend less on items and services you purchase on a regular basis. Are you ready?

# Chapter 2- Helpful Ways to Budget Money

As I mentioned in the previous chapter, there are many ways that people budget their money. I use a spreadsheet on my computer that fills in the blanks for me. However, there are other methods to budgeting that might work out better for your personality and spending habits. In this chapter, I'm going to give you some ways that people budget their money that helps them to save and still feel like they have their financial situation under control.

*Cash Envelopes*

Some people find that they spend less when they have cash on hand rather than using a credit or a debit card. Try putting money in an envelope before going out and only allow yourself to spend what is in that envelope. Once it is gone, you cannot spend any more. This will help you to not overspend just because you have the money in an account.

*Separate Bank Accounts*

In a day and age where getting a bank account is practically free, try splitting your money into accounts that are designated for that purpose will help you to put your money where it belongs as it comes in. Many online sites allow you to nickname your accounts, so having these accounts can be an easy way to put your money where it needs to be and take away the temptation of spending it right away.

*Writing it down as it Happens*

Even though many people don't balance a checkbook anymore, it is still a good practice. You may not even use checks, but carry around a checkbook register and record every time you spend money. This will give you a clear view of when and how your money is being spent. Once you understand where your money goes, you will be able to change how it's spent.

*Rounding Up*

This is one of my favorite ways to save a little extra money. Every time that I use my debit card, I will round the total up the next dollar. When I reconcile my statement at the end of the month, the money that I rounded up is put into a savings account that I have for vacations. This is a painless way to save money because it's basically saving less than a dollar a transaction!

*Change to the Piggy Bank*

This concept follows the same idea as the one with the debit card. With cash, instead of diving for that penny, allow the change to accumulate. When you arrive home, but that change in the piggy bank and allow it to build up for a while. After your container is full, take it to a Coin star or bank and have them count it for you! You may be surprised how much you can save with putting your change in a piggy bank!

*Computer Programs*

If you have a computer, you will more than likely have software that you can generate a budget spreadsheet on. Use your resources and give yourself a visual representation of what your budget looks like and find places where you can change it in order to see better results.

Budgeting isn't necessarily sitting down with a piece of paper and balancing every cent. It can be in the way that you look at spending, how you save your money before it's spent, and how you handle the surplus or deficit. Many people get stressed out when the idea of budgeting comes into play because they feel that it will be like an amateur accounting job. Don't think about it in that way. Think about it as a way to understand where your money goes and why your finances look like they do once you reach the end of the month.

Once you change your views on budgeting, it will be a much easier task. You might even find that finding ways to spend less and save money can be fun! Money shouldn't have to be stressful, even though it's necessary to survive.

# Chapter 3- Creative Ways to Save Money

It may be hard to save money, especially when you feel like you won't have anything left once you pay all the bills. However, if you take a look at the small things you can do to spend less, you will find that you can save money for a rainy day. Saving money is not easy, but it is possible if you practice self-control and know that the money you are saving will serve a good purpose.

For some, having a typical savings account isn't enough. If the money is there, it's easy to spend. While this might be the most conventional and easiest way to save money, it is also the easier way to access your saved money and use it up before you realize it. Let's take a look at some ways you can creatively put money aside so that you don't spend it before you achieve your savings goals.

*Make a Contest to See How Much You Can Save on a Specific Item*

If you're a competitive person, you will enjoy this suggestion. Even if you're competing against yourself, you can still make this work for you. Try to find bargains on items that you buy and use on a regular basis. The less expensive you can find it, the more points you earn. Take away the sale price from the normal retail price and see how much you saved. The more you save, the better. I love doing this as a family. I shop at one grocery store and my husband will go to another. As we shop, we will see which store has the better price on which products. The person who can find the most savings is the winner.

*Finding as Many Coupons as Possible*

Coupons are a wonderful way to save money instantly. By taking the time to find retailer and manufacturer coupons, you could be saving on an item that is already discounted. Clipping and finding coupons can be a time consuming venture, but the money that it saves can be astounding. You don't have to be an extreme couponer in order to make coupons work for you and save you a lot of money. Just use what you can find when you find them. On average, I tend to save a hundred dollars each grocery shopping trip because I can find coupons and in store specials that add up to great savings.

*Savings Jar with a Savings Thermometer*

You will see this method when people are saving in schools or in jobs for the benefit of a fundraiser. Why not make your savings a fundraiser within itself? Set up a jar that you can put extra cash and change in. After adding your money, fill in the thermometer to reflect how much is in that jar. For example, if you're saving for a vacation, you may have an end goal on your thermometer that will tell you that you have saved enough money to meet the expenses. This can be an exciting way for everyone to see how well your savings is coming along and get them excited for the end goal.

*Have a Piggy Bank Competition*

Kids love this. It helps them to learn how to save. Give each of your children a piggy bank that they are responsible for putting money in. Have a time frame and make sure that the child cannot see into the piggy bank. After the time period has elapsed, empty the banks and see who has saved the most money. You can then take the money saved and put it into a savings account at the bank and let it stay there.

*Find Savings in Unusual Places*

You may be surprised at some of the places that savings will show itself. By going online before you shop or purchase services, you might be able to find savings in some obscure places. It will take some time and investigation on your part to find the savings and make sure they are legitimate, but you more than likely will stand to find something that you can use!

*Learning Where to Save*

Even though two retailers sell the same product does not mean that they have the same prices. For example, grocery stores have reputations for being the "expensive" store or the "cheap" store. After shopping at a few stores, find which store typically offers you the best deals and shop there. Even though another store might have a better price on one item doesn't mean that shopping there will save you money in the long run. You're looking for a place that will consistently offer you lower prices, even though you may pay more for just one item.

*Treasure Stashes*

When I was a child, my mother had a habit of stashing money away in the house for a rainy day. She called them her treasure stashes because she sometimes surprised herself when she came across the money. It had been so well hidden that she forgot that she had even placed it there! This could be a good way to save if you are slightly forgetful and have extra cash to save. It can also be fun to find stashes that you have forgotten existed!

*Listing the Pros and Cons Prior to Purchase*

For major purchases, take the time and list the positive and negative aspects of the purchase. Do you really need it? Can you find it at a better price? Will another brand accomplish the same goals for less? By analyzing your purchase before you make it, you will either find out how good of an idea it is, or you will find out if you can live without it. Just taking the time to think about it can save you the money!

Finding creative ways to save money can be both fun and rewarding. Also, making saving a family project gets everyone involved and teaches your children the value of saving for the future. It might take a while for you to save the amount of money you wish to save, but it will add up over time and you will be able to see the benefits in the future. Spending less and saving more can be fun and teach you and your family the value of a dollar.

# Chapter 4- Learning to Investigate Purchases

With as much competition as there is out there for places to sell their merchandise, someone will have a lower price than the first place you turn to. While looking at your item online and in stores can be time consuming, saving extra money will be worth it in the end. Stores take advantage of the fact that it's convenient just to buy what they have to offer. They don't take into account that the competitor may be offering a much better price for the same item.

By taking the time to research and investigate potential purchases online and in store, you are preparing yourself to get the best price. You will also be exposing yourself to deals and specials that may not be evident in the ads that are posted in the newspaper and online. Just a little extra time can save you a whole lot of extra money!

*Cell Phone Apps*

With the advent of smartphones, there have been tons of wonderful apps that can help you save. If you can't make it to a computer to do your comparison shopping, pull up your app store and find a few highly rated apps that can help you to make an informed decision. You can find apps about where to find the cheapest gas, the cheapest tickets, or whatever else you wish to purchase. In a few moments, you smartphone can save you a bundle. Thank you, smartphone!

*Comparison Websites*

There are a ton of websites out there that will give you the prices of different places selling what you are looking to buy.

These have recently become popular for airline tickets and travel, but you can find them for almost anything that you are shopping for. Take the time and see who is selling what you want for the best price and go from there. Just because it's convenient doesn't meant that it is the best purchase for you. Do your research!

*Price Match Guarantees*

A lot of stores want your business, and they will offer you a price match guarantee if you can prove that another retailer is selling the same item for a cheaper price. However, you have to be careful with some of these policies. Some places won't honor prices that are contingent upon a shopper's card. However, if you find a sale price that you feel you can price match, it doesn't hurt to try!

*Online Prices*

When shopping, the retailer's online price is often less than what you can purchase it for in the store. Also, there might be an online sale for that item that isn't honored in the store. If you like instant gratification, then get over it. If it's cheaper online, wait for it to be shipped and purchase it there. This, of course, goes for an item that isn't needed immediately.

*Checking for Sales*

Stores change their sales periodically. Some may change them weekly or biweekly. Figure out the sales of the stores that you shop and when they are due to change. When the new sales come out, check up on them right away and see if you can find some good savings that you can stock up on. Stocking up on products when they are on sale is a great way to save money, granted that the items are not perishable.

*Buy Used if Possible*

When it comes to some items, you might be able to find what you're looking for at a thrift store and save yourself a lot of money. Buying used clothing and other goods is not shameful, but smart. People are constantly upgrading and getting rid of the old, so by taking advantage of this, you could find items that are nearly new at a fraction of the cost!

*Wait if Necessary*

Things will eventually go on sale. If you find that you want to purchase something but it is too expensive, wait it out a little while. Either the store will mark down the price, or the price will drop on its own. Even if you don't get what you want when it's extremely popular, you can still enjoy the benefits of it at a later date!

*Call Ahead to Confirm*

When stores have sales, the items sometimes sell out quickly, especially when they are at the end of the sale. Don't waste your time by going to the store to purchase these items without calling and checking their availability before you leave home. It can be a wasted trip if you show up to find that they sold out of what you intended to purchase days before. All stores have a way you can contact them, so don't be afraid to make use of this resource.

The goal to having a great budget and spending less is knowing how to work the system. People are so set on being instantly gratified by purchases that they often spend much more than they would if they were to wait just a few days. Don't be that type of person. Allow yourself to be patient and wait for the best opportunity to buy. Your budget and your wallet will be smiling at you later on!

# Chapter 5- The Trick to Finding a Creative Budget

Spending less money is just one way to get your budget to have a positive figure at the end of the month. Knowing what you can spend and monitoring how you spend your money can really help you see what your spending habits are and how they can be changed in order to ensure that you are saving rather than spending. If a traditional budget just isn't cutting it for you, then there are other ways to budget your money and still reap the same benefits of a traditional budget.

You may have seen seminars done on ways to budget that have saved people money by thinking outside the typical spending habits that we are used to today. In this chapter, I want to take a look at some of these creative budgeting methods and how they can help you to save your hard earned money for what you really want to spend it on. I also want to add a couple of other ideas that will help you get into the saving mindset.

*Money Envelope Method*

This method has been extremely successful for many people. The concept is that you use cash for everything. Having the cash in hand, you divide the money into specific envelopes that are devoted to certain bills. For example, you will have an envelope for your rent, the car payment, groceries, or whatever else you have that is a regular expense. You are limited to the money in that envelope. If you run out of grocery money, then you must wait until the next round of budgeting comes around. The envelope method has taught people the importance of watching what they spend and spending their money a little more wisely.

*Money Jars*

Money jars follow along the same concept, except they are used for saving. Set up for jars, one for vacation, one for outings, one for extras, and whatever else you could use extra money for. Put the spare cash and coins from your money envelopes into these jars and allow the money to accumulate. You are not only using a great way to track your spending, you are also saving for something that you can have fun doing!

*Daily Savings Method*

I have seen this suggestion around the holidays in regards to having gift money. What happens is, you save a dollar (or whatever denomination you want) the first day, two dollars the second day, and so forth, doubling the amount daily or weekly. This money is then put into savings to fund whatever you wish to use it for. The idea is that by the end of a time period, your money has drastically multiplied and you have saved more than you could by other methods.

*Budget Box*

A budget box is a way that is similar to money envelopes. With the box, you save each receipt and each bill you paid and it is filed under its personalized category. At the end of the month, you will pull out your receipts and analyze what you spent your money on and where. This is a good way to catch unnecessary spending/

*Monthly Savings Plan*

Having a set amount that you put into your savings account on a monthly basis will help you to mentally part with that money before it's even in your hands. I like to put a certain percentage of my paycheck into my savings account and work with the rest of it when I budget. By taking this money out first, I am not planning on using it, and the budget will be centered on the rest of the paycheck.

## Meals on the Cheap

This is a fun method that I came across online and have just started to use recently. What you do is, you go grocery shopping and buy your meat and vegetables in bulk. These meats and vegetables need to be able to be frozen because you are going to store a good portion of what you buy in the freezer. Once you have found your meat and vegetables at a bargain, you will prepare it in bulk for several meals. For example, you will have enough taco meat that you can make tacos and nachos for two different meals. By preparing your food at once, you save yourself both time and money.

## Teaching Children to Save

Since we live in a time where savings is not emphasized, teaching your children how to save young will prepare them to save as adults. When they are old enough to understand what saving is, take them and give them their own savings account at the bank. Then when they have extra money, take them to the bank with you and let them deposit it. This will teach them not only about saving, but it will teach them how to bank.

## Eliminating Unnecessary Spending

We all have a vice that we spend money unnecessarily on. Coffee is mine. I know I have used it as an example a few times in this book. I love coffee. Not just any coffee, but fancy coffee that you buy at coffee shops. However, this coffee is expensive. In order to eliminate that unnecessary expense, I have learned to find creamers and other additives to make my coffee fancy at home. This saves me money daily, and I can get almost the same effects as my barista did.

Learning different methods to saving and budgeting can be incredibly helpful, especially if you have a very limited income. Having a good concept of what you are spending and how you can save will help you to build a good mindset on what money is and where it goes in your life.

# Chapter 6- Looking Forward to the Future

Our society has become one of spenders rather than savers. We haven't seen the true effects of this change yet, but once we begin to get older, our generation is going to struggle to survive. This could be due to the fact that retirement and our futures seem so far away that we would rather live in the moment now. However, if you take time to think about where you will be when you hit retirement age, you may not like the picture that is presented to you.

Saving is an important aspect in ensuring that we will survive once we hit retirement age. Learning how to save now when our society is telling us to spend can really influence your future as a senior citizen. Just think about this as I give you some ways on how saving now can vastly influence your retirement.

*401K Plans*

Many employers offer 401K plans that help their employees to put a portion of their money into the stock market and help them save for retirement. This is simply a deduction from your paycheck, and it is put into an account that will sit there for years. When you leave a job, if your 401K isn't large enough, they will disperse it to you or give you the option to roll it over into your new employer's plan. It is encouraged that you roll it over so that you don't suffer the tax penalties and you can continue to save for your retirement.

*IRAs*

Alongside 401K's, employers may also offer you an IRA (Individual Retirement Account). These accounts save a portion of your money for retirement and are kept at a bank, so they are insured like any other account. Again, if you leave your employer, depending on the type of IRA, you may be forced to roll it over or cash it out. Also, you as an individual can set up your own personal IRA and contribute to it. This allows you to continuously save.

*Investments*

Aside from using employer retirement resources, you can choose to invest your money on your own. There are a number of different types of investments you can make that will help you to grow your money for retirement. While some are risky, others are solid and can help you to gain a good increase. There are options such as the stock market or precious metals. You can find an investment that will feel comfortable for you and make it work for your retirement savings.

*Bonds*

Bonds are another great way to invest. It is essentially the government borrowing money from you. You have to wait a good period of time before your bond is matured, but once it is, you can make a profit off of the initial purchase price. Depending on when you purchase your bonds, the interest rates might be poor or good. Either way, the government will pay you interest for the loan that you are giving them!

*College Savings Plan*

For younger people who are planning on going to college and establishing a career, having a college savings plan will help them to set themselves up for the future. The habits that they use to save for college can be transferred later on in life to help them to understand the importance of saving and how it can benefit then for life. The younger that someone is taught to save, the more ingrained it will become into how they handle their finances.

*Retirement Calculators*

If you're a long ways away from being able to retire, then it might be to your benefit to look at a calculator of what experts believe will be your necessary expenses when you are ready to retire. No one can tell you with one hundred percent certainty what the world will look like in ten or twenty years, but they can predict what it will be like. By taking this information and planning ahead, you stand a better chance of saving enough money so that you can comfortably retire and not be required to work after retirement age. Also, we have to look at the fact that we may not benefit from social security like retirees today do. Take this into account when you set up a savings plan for your individual retirement.

Focusing on your future can help you when the time comes to retire, go to college, or even go on a family vacation. Just because you have money now does not mean that you will have that money in the future. Be wise in how you spend and think about how your spending habits can impact your future in positive of negative ways. Knowing your habits and your spending trends will help you to predict what your budget might look like in the future.

Don't be unprepared for what is to come. Take the time now to focus on saving and making sure that you have enough for your future plans. You will be grateful that you made these changes now, and you will be spending less now and loving it!

# Chapter 7- Spending Less, Saving More

It may seem silly to think that creating a budget could save your life. I'm not talking like a life-saving medicine, but it could save your lifestyle and your future plans. Once you start to think about how saving can really influence how you live, what you will have in the future, and making your dreams come true, you might think twice before purchasing that next coffee at the coffee shop.

The present really does affect the future. What you do now with your income and how you save it will ultimately affect your comfort levels when you retire, or even if you will have the ability to retire. It has become way too common for senior citizens to continue to work because their social security checks don't cover all of their expenses. Don't you want to be able to enjoy your retirement? That is just one reason to think about your spending and your savings right now, when you have the ability to change your spending habits.

Now that you know ways to budget and save your money, you are ready to make the necessary changes to ensure that you have the kind of future that you wish to live. Think about it as saving your life. In essence, you are saving your future from being one of poverty and not having enough to support yourself once you decide to retire.

Keep the tips that I have presented in this book in mind the next time that you get ready to swipe a card on an impulse buy. Will that impulse buy make it so that you are one less meal in your older years? It might be crazy to think about it in this respect, but knowing that it can mean the difference of food on the table as a senior citizen may change your mind and influence you to put that purchase back.

Once I realized how saving money really could affect my life, I am happy to make the small and even the big changes in the way that I budget and save my money. I know that when I am of retirement age, I will actually get to retire. However, I really had to start that savings plan as a young adult. It will be years before I can retire, but knowing that I won't have to depend on someone to take care of my financial needs makes me love spending less and saving.

I really hope that you too will find that you will love saving money and budgeting. Spending less now can lead to a full and fulfilling future!

# Conclusion

I hope this book was able to help you to find some conventional and creative ways to learn how to budget and save your money by spending less. In a society where we don't think about how we spend money, getting into a habit of saving and budgeting can be beneficial to your future financial success.

The next step is to try some of the suggestions that I have made in this book and see what works for you. Once you get into the habit of spending less and saving, you will find that you love the results!

# FRUGAL MINIMALISM
## And Loving It

### 50 Proven Steps To Live A Minimalist Lifestyle, Clear Your Clutter And Live With Less

**KATHY STANTON**

# Introduction

This book contains proven steps and strategies on how to make changes in your life to live a frugal minimalist lifestyle and live your life clutter free.

Each chapter in this book will help you make all of the changes needed in order to help you live a minimalist lifestyle. You will find numerous tips and strategies that you can start doing right now to change your life, live a clutter free life and reduce the stress in your life.

You will learn how removing the clutter from your home can save you money as well as time. You will also learn how to not only remove the clutter from your home, but from your entire life in order to be happier and stress free.

By the time you finish this book you will understand how adapting to the minimalist lifestyle will help you focus on what is really important to you and your family by removing what is taking away from your core values.

© **Copyright 2019 by _____Kathy Stanton_____ - All rights reserved.**

This document is geared towards providing exact and reliable information in regards to the topic and issue covered. The publication is sold with the idea that the publisher is not required to render accounting, officially permitted, or otherwise, qualified services. If advice is necessary, legal or professional, a practiced individual in the profession should be ordered.

- From a Declaration of Principles which was accepted and approved equally by a Committee of the American Bar Association and a Committee of Publishers and Associations.

In no way is it legal to reproduce, duplicate, or transmit any part of this document in either electronic means or in printed format. Recording of this publication is strictly prohibited and any storage of this document is not allowed unless with written permission from the publisher. All rights reserved.

The information provided herein is stated to be truthful and consistent, in that any liability, in terms of inattention or otherwise, by any usage or abuse of any policies, processes, or directions contained within is the solitary and utter responsibility of the recipient reader. Under no circumstances will any legal responsibility or blame be held against the publisher for any reparation, damages, or monetary loss due to the information herein, either directly or indirectly.

Respective authors own all copyrights not held by the publisher.

The information herein is offered for informational purposes solely, and is universal as so. The presentation of the information is without contract or any type of guarantee assurance.

The trademarks that are used are without any consent, and the publication of the trademark is without permission or backing by the trademark owner. All trademarks and brands within this book are for clarifying purposes only and are the owned by the owners themselves, not affiliated with this document.

# Chapter 1
# An Introduction to the Minimalist Lifestyle

What does it mean to live a minimalist lifestyle? It means that you try to live your life with only the things that you need. Living a frugal lifestyle means that you live in a way so that you are not wasting and spending as little as possible. If you want to become a frugal minimalist, you will be living your life with the things that you need in a way that is not wasting and saving you money.

Many people have the wrong idea when it comes to living a minimalist lifestyle. They think of someone who is not eating enough food, they don't use their electricity, they dress in clothing that went out of fashion in the 1970's and live a boring life.

Although this may be true in some cases, it is not true in all of them. It really depends on how far you want to take the lifestyle and what you are willing to give up. For example, if you have no need for clothes that are in today's fashion then you may give that up. If however your job calls for you to look professional, a 1981 floral dress may not be the best option for you.

At its core, minimalism is simply focusing on the things we love the most in our lives and removing the things that take our focus off of what we love. Minimalism also frees you from the obsession that so many people are suffering with today and that is the obsession of possessions.

When you live a minimalist lifestyle, you do not worry about keeping up with the Jones', you simply worry about what will benefit you the most in your life. Many of us have been led to believe that in order to live the good life we must have as many possessions as possible. The truth is that most of these possessions serve no purpose and end up taking time away from the things we love the most.

Being a minimalist does not mean that you have to come home to an empty house with no furniture. It does not mean that you sleep on a mat on the floor with a few blankets. What it means is that you do not accumulate so much stuff that the stuff begins taking away from your quality of life.

Living a minimalist lifestyle allows us to take a step back from the hustle of life. Today we rush from one meeting to another, our evenings are filled with activities, we eat on the go and if we are lucky we are able to spend a few minutes with our families and then squeeze in a few hours of sleep.

Minimalism allows you to walk away from that lifestyle and slow down. You will be free from the modern thinking that multitasking is always best and that your schedule should always be full. You will keep the significant tasks in your life but remove the things which cause a hindrance. In doing so, you will actually be able to add value to your life.

Many people believe that living a minimalist lifestyle has only to do with possessions. However, being a minimalist is more internal than it is external. When you first start out and through much of this book we are going to focus on the external. Then once the decluttering is done and your life begins to become more balanced, you will be able to focus on the internal issues that need working on.

For example, have you ever asked yourself why you insist on purchasing every single magnet you come across? These are the deeper issues that you will be able to focus on once you have handled all of the external issues. When you are able to spend time dealing with the deeper issues you will live a much happier life.

You can reach your goals of living a minimalist lifestyle. I know right now you may be looking around and thinking how am I ever going to figure this out? How will I ever accomplish this? And I am assuming that is why you purchased this book. I like so many others are living proof that becoming a minimalist is possible and that you can be a frugal minimalist, living a happier life than you ever thought was possible.

Throughout the rest of this book we are going to go over specific areas of your life that you can begin focusing on. We are going to discuss things that you can do right now in your life to move towards a minimalist lifestyle. When you finish with this book, and complete all of the tasks in it, you will have completely decluttered not only your home, but your entire life. You will be living a much happier life than you are right now.

Beginning with the external clutter and issues will encourage you to move the idea of living a minimalist lifestyle to every area of your life. Remember it is not all about getting rid of your possessions, it is about the principles of the lifestyle which we will talk more about as we work our way through this book.

# Chapter 2
# How to Get Rid of the Clutter in Your Home

As you look around your house it may seem like the job of removing the clutter is just far too great. You may feel like you just cannot part with your belongings. I remember when I first began, I looked around my home and thought there was no way I was getting rid of anything. After all, I had spent my money that I earned and worked hard for to purchase the things I owned.

Then I read an article that talked about how much time I was spending on the items I had already purchased. You see, not only did each item I purchased cost me money which was in reality time out of my life, but it was literally costing me money each day.

Now think about all of the items you have. How much time are you spending on them? Isn't there something you would much rather be doing with that time? That is what made me decide I was going to start on the road of decluttering.

1. Start in one room, if one room seems to be too much, start in one corner. One of the main reasons why people do not start the process of removing clutter is because they are overwhelmed with the process. They look around and see that so much needs to be done, then they give up before they ever start. Instead of failing before you begin, you need to pick an area and start small. You can pick a drawer in the kitchen or the bathroom cabinets. Whatever area you choose to start with make sure you focus on getting rid of all of the things you don't need and organizing the things you keep.

2. Get four boxes, one labeled donate, one sell, one keep and one throw away. As you go through each of your items, you need to ask yourself if this is something you really need? Ask yourself if it is going to enrich your life or if it is going to take away from your life? If you really do not need the item it will either go in the sell, donate or throw away box. If you need it, then it will go in the keep box, after you clean it. If the item is going to take away from your life, it will go in either the sell, donate or throw away box. And if you can sell it, then the item will go in the sell box. If you cannot sell the item, place it in the donate box unless it is broken then you will throw it away.

Once you have all three boxes full, you will clean the area in which you are planning to place all of your keep items. Then throw away your trash, either post your sale items on Facebook or keep them for a yard sale and donate your donate box. Move on to the next area of the home and repeat this process.

3. One thing that causes a lot of people issues is when they come across items that have been left to them by members of their family that have passed. Many people feel obligated to hold on to these items and feel guilty if they consider getting rid of them. You will need to ask yourself is that is really what your family member wanted? Would they want you to become overwhelmed by their belongings or would they prefer that you live well? I am going to guess that they would prefer you live well.

One rule of thumb that I like to use is that you can keep one item from each family member that has passed. It can be something that was meaningful to you or to them. In some cases it is okay to keep two or three items as long as they are not huge, but you should never have a houseful of a family member or friend who has passed on. This will not allow you to grieve and will only cause you more pain.

One example of this is that when my grandfather passed I was grief stricken, after I realized what I was doing with his belongings, I chose to keep two items. One was a clock because he used to collect them and the other was the first thing I ever bought for him when I got my first job. These two items had meaning for me. I allowed the rest of the family to take what they wanted and donated the rest of the items.

You need to remember that just because you remove the item from your home, it does not mean you are removing your memories of the person. If you feel the need to, you can take pictures of the items and keep the pictures. Pictures take up much less space than a lifetime of items that a person has collected.

4. Stop buying things. While you are in the process of decluttering your home, stop purchasing new items. One exception to this is that you can purchase organizational items such as bins or shelves. Do not purchase anything else. If you do find an item that you feel you have to purchase, remember that when you get home you have to get rid of one of the items in your home.

5. This brings us to one in one out. Whenever you purchase one item, you need to remove one item from your home. This will help to ensure that your home does not become over run with clutter again.

6. No more impulse purchases. When you see something you want, leave it at the store and write it down. If you still want the item in 30 days then you can go ahead and purchase it. Most of the time you will completely forget about the item and save yourself some money!

7. Don't save items that you may need one day. Many of us get caught up in thinking that we might need an item some day and telling ourselves that we are actually saving money by keeping these items. Instead sell or donate the item and put the money in the bank. This way you don't have to worry about keeping track of an item that you may use one day. Most of the time when we keep items like this, we forget we have them and

lose track of where they are. Then we end up purchasing a new item anyway.

8. If an item is not needed to live, ask yourself if you really love the item. If the answer is yes, then keep it, if the answer is no then sell it or donate the item.

9. Instead of adding another broken item to your to fix list, fix it now. Think about how many things you are planning to fix. If you have an item that has been broken for more than a month and you have lived without it. then throw it away. If you need to fix something in your house such as your cabinet doors, do it now and try to stop putting it off.

And finally if you have items that need fixed that you cannot live without, fix them as soon as they break instead of continuing to put it off. If you can put off repairing the item, you don't need it.

10. Think about all of the things you will be able to do in your new found clutter free space. What types of things will you and your family do in your home once it is clutter free? This is where values come into play when you become a minimalist. When you choose to become a minimalist, you are choosing to put the things that you value most in your life and get rid of the things that interfere with what you value.

It may seem overwhelming at first, but remember you will be able to remove the clutter from your home with patience and hard work. It may take some time but everything that is worth doing does take time. Remember that you did not accumulate all of the clutter overnight and you are not going to be able to get rid of it all over night!

One thing that I have found is that clutter attracts clutter and when you have space you will be more likely to create more space. One warning I like to give is to not get rid of too much stuff. One person I was working with removed everything from their home that they did not need to live. This included pictures off of the walls, plants out of the house and even the television.

They found that they were depressed and bored when they went into their home and did not enjoy life like they once did. Do not remove everything from your home. The point is to create a comfortable environment that is not overrun by clutter for you and your family.

# Chapter 3
# How to Have a Minimalist Wardrobe

I talked earlier a little bit about how many people thought that in order to be a minimalist they had to dress frumpy and out of style, but that is just not true. Deciding to use a minimalist wardrobe simply means that you no longer have to go into your closet and stand there overwhelmed trying to figure out what to wear. You no longer have to worry about what matches what because everything goes together and you know exactly what you own.

Many people will think that this is impossible but it really is not. The fact is that you only need a few outfits instead of hundreds of them. You also do not need 50 or more pairs of shoes. In this chapter I am going to show you exactly how you can accomplish this.

11. Choose 2 to 3 pairs of pants to wear during the week. These need to be versatile. Many people choose to just have one pair of black pants. I prefer to have at least two pair of pants in case something happens and I need to wear pants two days in a row but am not able to do laundry one night. I also like to have one pair of blue jeans as well.

12. Five shirts of different colors are great to have also, but you don't want the colors to be too different. For example if you like brown you don't want a bright pink shirt as well.

13. That brings us to color. You want to choose a basic color. One that is neutral, brown, black or khaki is great. You need to find one that works with your skin

color and hides stains well. For me my basic color is brown. I make sure that I do not get an ugly brown but one that is pretty and looks good on me.

14. Fit is the next thing you need to think about. You don't want to keep clothes that are too tight hoping that one day you will be able to fit into them. You don't want to wear clothes that are too big for you because this just makes you look slouchy. If you really want to make a minimalist wardrobe work you need to focus on fit.

15. Limit the color of your accessories. For example my purse is black and my flats are black, so is my coat. Any jewelry I have is silver so that everything always goes together.

16. You should also limit the amount of jewelry you have. 3 pair of earrings, a couple necklaces, a few bracelets, rings and a watch. Any more than that is just clutter.

17. You will also need a dress, and a black skirt. If you want to purchase a sweater to go over any short sleeved shirts you can do that as well. This helps bring a lot of versatility to your wardrobe and are a great investment.

18. You should make sure you have a workout outfit as well. Include a pair of good tennis shoes. You can be as creative as you want when it comes to the color of your work out outfit since you will only be working out in it.

19. I also like to ensure I have an outfit I can wear to clean the house in because I do not want to get bleach on my work clothes. This is simply a pair of comfortable yoga pants and a t-shirt for me, but can be whatever you choose.

20. Mix and match. Make sure that whatever you keep can be paired with any of the other items. You also want to make sure that there is nothing to formal and nothing to casual. For example, you can wear any of the items

you have to work or you can just as easily wear them to the grocery store or the neighbor's barbecue.

That is all it takes to create a minimalist wardrobe and have outfits that you can wear each day no matter where you are going. It does take a little bit of will power to get rid of the items you do not need. However once it is done and you find you don't have piles and piles of laundry to do each week and you don't have to face the daunting task of picking out your outfits each day, you will see that you are not only saving money but time as well.

# Chapter 4
# Minimalist Eating

Another thing I touched on a little bit earlier is the way a minimalist eats. Many people believe that a minimalist will barely eat anything, go out and scavenge for food or live off of rice. That does not have to be true.

You see one of the reasons so many people are afraid to become minimalists is because they do not have the correct information. I remember a few years ago I met a lady who was pale and sickly looking. She ate mostly food that she found or that was given to her. The problem was that she was not saving any money and she was causing herself to become sick.

As a minimalist you should eat healthy meals, eat until you are full and not go without.

21. Focus on not wasting! One of the main goals of being a minimalist is that we do not use more than you actually need. A lot of people purchase tons of food and let it go to waste. They don't save their leftovers to use later but instead throw them away. One of the most important things you can do when you are learning how to live a minimalist lifestyle is put leftovers in the fridge and heat them up later. These can be used as brown bagged lunches for work, or you can keep them and once a week have a leftover buffet dinner.

My family loves it when we have a buffet Sunday each week and they are able to choose from all of the foods we ate throughout the week. This also saves me a ton on my grocery bill. You also need to make sure you are not wasting your condiments, such as ketchup. Simply turn the bottle upside down and let all of the bits of ketchup drip down to the bottom. This way you will be able to get at least one extra serving out of each bottle.

To get more out of your barbeque sauce just add a bit of water to the bottle, shake it up and pour over your food.

22. Another thing that happens when you decide to eat like a minimalist is that you tend to eat healthier than you were before. Minimalists try to not spend their money on processed foods that provide no nutritional value, but instead eat an abundance of fresh fruits and vegetables. They also eat a lot of fresh fish and other meat.

   Many people think that it is more expensive to purchase healthy foods than it is to purchase processed foods. However, part of being frugal and learning to live a minimalist lifestyle is learning how to purchase healthy foods at a lower cost than processed foods. It is also about learning how to prepare these foods into delicious meals that you and your family can enjoy.

23. Choose to eliminate unhealthy foods from your diet. This means that you will be drinking a lot more water instead of drinking soda or other sugary drinks. Choose

to eliminate white breads, pasta and other processed foods. Eat only foods that provide the most nutritional value for the calories. If the food does not provide nutritional value, don't eat it.

24. It is not about eating bland or tasteless meals. This is where a lot of people get confused. You don't have to eat boiled chicken with lettuce and rice every night. It does not taste good and it is not healthy. Our bodies need nutrients in order to work, they need fat and we need flavor to enjoy our food. Don't feel as if you have to give up taste in order to be frugal and live as a minimalist.

25. It is not about eating a low calorie diet or counting calories. It is about giving your body the fuel it needs in order to function properly. It is about eating until you are full, but not gorging yourself on foods that do your body no good. It is not even about never eating chocolate cake again, but doing so in a way that does not waste food or harm your body.

26. You will have to become organized when it comes to eating if you want to be frugal and still live a minimalist lifestyle. Each week you will need to sit down and plan out all of your meals. You will need to focus on what is on sale and what you like. You don't have to give up your comfort foods that you regularly enjoy, but you need to focus on nutrients.

27. Avoid snacking especially when it comes to junk food or vending machines. You do not want to waste your money on vending machines, so make sure that you take enough food with you when you go to work so you are not tempted by a vending machine. If you need a snack try to eat a piece of fruit. This may be difficult at first if you are used to eating sweet or salty foods, but it does get easier. You can also try to snack on nuts when you find them on sale.

28. Cut back on your portion sizes. One thing that I learned very quickly was that the larger our plates are the large portion sizes we use. Use a smaller plate and you will find that you are eating less and wasting less as well. When we use a large plate we fill it up whether we will eat it or not then when we do not eat all of the food we throw it away. Instead when you use a smaller plate you will not have as much left and chances are you will leave nothing on your plate.

29. Don't go back for seconds. When you go back for seconds you will generally over fill your plate and this food again goes to waste. Instead, make sure you have the food you want the first time, make your plate, put the leftovers away and eat what you serve yourself. If you get hungry later, grab a small portion or eat a piece of fruit.

30. Minimize going out to eat. You should cut back as much as possible when it comes to going out to eat. When you do go out to eat, split one meal between two people. The portion sizes of most meals that are served at restaurants are much larger than what is really needed and can easily be split between 2 people. Simply ask for an extra plate when ordering.

# Chapter 5
# How to Declutter Your Life and Finances

I spoke earlier about how becoming a minimalist was not only about removing the clutter from your home, but was about removing the clutter from your life. In this chapter I want to focus on how you can remove the clutter from your finances.

31. Start by making a list of all of your bills. Each bill that you have to pay each month whether it be a necessity or a luxury. After all of your bills are listed, decide which ones you can get rid of. For example, can you mow your lawn yourself or dry clean your own clothes? After you pick which luxuries you can get rid of start removing them right away.

32. Cut back on the bills you have to pay. For example instead of paying $100 per month for cable services, consider ending that service and purchasing Netflix for $8 a month or some service like it. Instead of paying $200 a month for your cell phone with internet, purchase a $20 prepaid smart phone and cut your bill back to 40 dollars a month.

33. Start paying off debt. One of the goals of a minimalist is to live debt free. The only way you will reach this goal is to start paying off your debt right now. Make a list of all that you owe. Start with the debt that is the smallest and instead of paying the minimum on this bill pay a little extra each month, as much as you can afford. For example, if your minimum payment on your credit card that you owe the least to is $40 a month, pay $80 instead. Once this bill is paid off, use that $80 plus

whatever you were paying toward the next smallest debt and continue until all of your debt is paid off.

34. Do not accrue more debt. Cut up the credit cards and stop digging yourself deeper into the debt hole. If you cannot cut up the credit cards, you can put them in a cup of water and freeze them. When you are tempted to use them you are going to have to wait for them to thaw out which will give you the opportunity to consider if you really want to add more debt to what you already have.

35. Simplify the number of checking and savings accounts you have. Instead of having multiple accounts, choose to only have one checking account and one savings account. Choose the checking account that offers the most benefits and the savings account that will provide the highest interest rate. Ask your banker which accounts will benefit you the most.

36. Track how much you are spending each month. How many times have you gotten to the end of the month and realized you have no money left, but you don't have any idea where it went? Start by writing down everything you purchase, no matter how small write it down. Keep a running list for an entire month and at the end of the month find out what you are spending your money on. Then you can change how you are spending your money.

37. Create a purchase price spread sheet. This spreadsheet is going to track the prices that you are willing to pay for the items you purchase. This will be the rock bottom price and you will want to track how often these prices come about. For example, if a can of corn is normally 89 cents but once every six months you can get them for 39 cents, you will track this sale and know when it is time to stock up and how much you will need to purchase. This may not seem like much, but if you

consider 10 cans of corn can save you $5 you will find that it really adds up.

38. Purchase used and save the difference. This is one thing that has helped me save a ton of money. I have purchased furniture, televisions, clothing, and even plants used. By doing so I have been able to save a ton of money. I actually bought a living room couch for $25. It is in perfect condition and has outlasted the couch I purchased new for a lot more than $25. This should also be applied when purchasing a car.

39. Consider using coupons. One thing that I like to do in order to save money and live a frugal lifestyle as well as be a minimalist is to use coupons to make my purchases. I am able to save anywhere from 70-100% with coupons on my purchases. You need to make sure that if you are using coupons you are not purchasing things that you would not normally purchase and that you do not end up hoarding items.

If for example you find an item that you would not use but can get it for free go ahead and get it, but make sure you give it to someone who can actually use it.

40. Try to avoid convenience purchases. Instead of purchasing a cup of coffee on the way to work, make it at home and take it with you. Instead of purchasing microwaveable meals, make your own. This is a great use for leftovers. Instead of going for convenience items it is much better for your finances if you avoid them.

# Chapter 6
# Gifts

This is another part of life that can cause a lot of clutter.

41. One way gifts can cause clutter in our lives and our homes is when people feel the need to constantly give us things. When you decide to adapt to a minimalist lifestyle, people will try to give you tons of stuff. They will want to give you home décor, clothing and tons of different items. You will have to explain to your friends and family that if they want to give you gifts, they need to give you something that you need not just things to sit around your home and fill up your space.

42. Birthdays and Christmas can cause issues as well. You don't want to deny your child toys as they are growing. Even though these are not needed in life, they help with a childs development. Before each holiday, take the time to go through your childs toys and remove any item that they have outgrown. Create a list for your family of acceptable items that can be purchased. There is nothing worse than having tons of $1 toys that no one plays with filling up toy boxes or breaking after the first use. Simply explain to your family that these items are not needed and give them the option to deposit a dollar in the child's savings account.

43. Gift giving is another issue that a minimalist has to face. There are those who have a gift closet. This is an area where they place items they have found on sale or have been given as a gift and use them for gifts later. I personally prefer to just give a gift card. This way the

gifts do not take up space in my home and I don't have to worry about wasting money on gifts that someone will not like.

44. What do you do about the gifts that have been given to you that you do not want or cannot use? Simply regift or donate them. Giving them to someone who is in need is much better than having them sit around your home and take up space!

Dealing with gifts is one of the easiest things when it comes to living a minimalist lifestyle. It is more difficult to explain to children the minimalist gifting changes that you will be making, but it does not take them too long to become accustom to the changes.

# Chapter 7
# Minimalist Living In Everyday Life

To finish up this book I want to go over a few things that really don't fit in any other section. Remember you don't have to make all of these changes all at once. This is a process and it is best that you choose one task to accomplish at a time, make one change in your life and once it becomes a habit for you then you can make the next change.

When you make changes in your life, it is normal to try and resist them. However if you make small changes, one at a time, it will make it much easier and less stressful.

45. Go through all of your emails and unsubscribe to any lists that you do not need to be part of. In just a little bit of time you can unsubscribe to 100 email lists and in the future, don't sign up for any lists that will not benefit you or that you will not read.

46. Go through your childs toys and get rid of the toys that they don't play with or that they have outgrown. If the child does not want to get rid of a toy allow them to keep it if it has sentimental meaning. If you find they want to keep everything, try explain to them that they can donate the toys to a child who does not have any toys.

47. Keep your home clean. Don't let the clutter start to take over again. Make sure you spend time each day to clean your home. Throw away the mail, don't let the magazines pile up and just take a few minutes to make sure you do not end up in the same situation you began with.

48. Don't keep anything on the kitchen counters that you do not use on a regular basis. Simply keeping the kitchen counters clean will encourage you to keep the rest of the house clean.

49. Fitness equipment can be something that many of us forget to deal with when it comes to dealing with clutter in our home. The reason for this is because we spend so much money purchasing the items that we plan on using someday. If you are not using the item right now, get rid of it. Consider doing other things to get your exercise. Instead of hoping that someday you will use the equipment, go outside and play with your kids today or if you don't have kids, take your dog for a walk.

50. Decorate your home for as little as possible. I talked a little bit about this when we discussed using second hand stores, but did you know that you can find tons of great items for cheap or even free by looking online or going to yard sales? Most of the things I have in my home as far as art or decorations go were obtained for free simply by looking for people who were willing to give things away.

Don't just rely on others to give things away. Each year I go through every item in our home and post an ad on Facebook listing all of the items I am giving away. I clear out the house and help others at the same time.

With all of the information I have given you in this book, you should be able to start living a frugal minimalist lifestyle, remove the clutter from your home and enjoy living a simpler lifestyle.

# Conclusion

I hope this book was able to help you to find ways that you can begin removing the clutter in your life and start living a minimalist lifestyle.

The next step is to choose one area in your life and focus on it. Set some minimalist goals and work toward them each day.

Finally, if you enjoyed this book, then I'd like to ask you for a favor, would you be kind enough to leave a review for this book on Amazon? It'd be greatly appreciated!

Click here to leave a review for this book on Amazon!

Thank you and good luck!

Printed in Great Britain
by Amazon